WILLIAM

POEMS

* ★ *

Selected and Introduced by Patti Smith

WILLIAM BLAKE was born in London in 1757. He was educated at home and then worked as an apprentice to the engraver James Basire before joining the Royal Academy in 1779. In 1782, he married Catherine Boucher and a year later began his career as a poet when he published *Poetical Sketches*. This was followed by *Songs of Innocence* (1789) and *Songs of Experience* (1794), which he also designed and engraved. His other major literary works include *The Book of Thel* (1789), *The Marriage of Heaven and Hell* (c. 1793), *Milton* (1804–8), and *Jerusalem* (1804–20). He produced many paintings and engravings during his lifetime. Blake died in 1827.

PATTI SMITH is a writer, performer, and visual artist. She gained recognition in the 1970s for her revolutionary merging of poetry and rock. She has released twelve albums, including *Horses*, which has been hailed as one of the top one hundred albums of all time by *Rolling Stone*. Smith had her first exhibit of drawings at the Gotham Book Mart in 1973 and has been represented by the Robert Miller Gallery since 1978. Her books include *M Train*, *Just Kids* (winner of the National Book Award), *Witt*, *Babel*, *Woolgathering*, *The Coral Sea*, and *Auguries of Innocence*. In 2005, the French Ministry of Culture awarded Smith the title of Commandeur de l'Ordre des Arts et des Lettres, the highest honor given to an artist by the French Republic. She was inducted into the Rock and Roll Hall of Fame in 2007. Smith married the musician Fred Sonic Smith in 1980. They had a son, Jackson, and a daughter, Jesse. Smith resides in New York City.

POEMS

POEMS

★ ★ ★

William Blake

Selected and Introduced by Patti Smith

VINTAGE CLASSICS
Vintage Books
A Division of Penguin Random House LLC
New York

FIRST VINTAGE CLASSICS EDITION, NOVEMBER 2016

Introduction and selection copyright © 2007 by Patti Smith

The text of this edition follows the versions established by
Geoffrey Keynes, which keep William Blake's own
spellings and capitalizations.

Library of Congress Cataloging-in-Publication Data
Names: Blake, William, 1757–1827, author. | Smith, Patti.
Title: Poems / William Blake ; selected and introduced by Patti Smith.
Description: First Vintage Classics edition. | New York :
Vintage Books, 2016. | Series: Vintage classics
Identifiers: LCCN 2016035734 | ISBN 9781101973141 (paperback)
Subjects: | BISAC: POETRY / English, Irish, Scottish, Welsh.
Classification: LCC PR4142.S55 2016 | DDC 821/.7—dc23 LC record
available at https://lccn.loc.gov/2016035734

Vintage Books Trade Paperback ISBN: 978-1-101-97314-1

www.vintagebooks.com

Printed in the United States of America
10   9   8   7   6   5   4   3   2   1

CONTENTS

From the Letters of William Blake:

INTRODUCTION

The eternal loom spins the immaculate word. The word forms the pulp and sinew of innocence. A newborn cries as the cord is severed, seeming to extinguish memory of the miraculous. Thus we are condemned to stagger rootless upon the earth in search for our fingerprint on the cosmos.

William Blake never let go of the loom's golden skein. The celestial source stayed bright within him, the casts of heaven moving freely in his sightline. He was the loom's loom, spinning the fiber of revelation; offering songs of social injustice, the sexual potency of nature, and the blessedness of the lamb. The multiple aspects of woven love.

His angels entreat, drawing him through the natural aspects of their kingdom into the womb of prophecy. He dips his ladle into the spring of inspiration, the flux of creation.

A rough-hewn seer who never tasted but English air, who loved Michelangelo yet never saw Rome.

Laboring over his work in sleeves ink-stained, he transfigures London into the new Jerusalem. His crushed hat and threadbare coat seem to pulsate as he wends his way through the grimy clatter. He heads past dark factories where pubescent girls with hair of matted gold offer themselves in the shadows for a bit of bread. Later, through his swift fingers, they transform as the virgins of his glad day, languishing in the bath of absolution, readied to accept the seed of God.

He is a messenger and a god himself. Deliverer, receptacle and fount.

★   ★   ★

My mother gave me Blake. In a church bazaar she found *Songs of Innocence*, a lovely 1927 edition faithful to the original. I spent long hours deciphering the calligraphy and contemplating the illustrations entwined with the text. I was fascinated by the possibility that one creates both word and image as did Blake, with copperplate, linen and rag, walnut oils, a simple pencil.

My father helped me comprehend this childless man who seemed to me the ultimate friend of children, who bemoaned their fate as chimney sweeps, laborers in the mills, berating the exploitation of their innocence and beauty.

Through my life I have returned to him.

When Allen Ginsberg lay dying, I was among those who sat vigil by his bedside. I wandered into his library and randomly chose a book, a volume of Blake in blood-red binding. Each poem was deeply annotated in Allen's hand, just as Blake had annotated Milton. I could imagine these prolific, complex men discoursing; the angels, mute, admiring.

William Blake felt that all men possessed visionary power. He cited from Numbers 11:29: 'Would to God that all the Lord's people were prophets.' He did not jealously guard his vision; he shared it through his work and called upon us to animate the creative spirit within us.

Nature sits on her throne, and science cannot contain her, just as religion cannot contain God. Nature sees naught of good and evil; one eye art, the other science.

*   *   *

'I wrote my happy songs, every child may joy to hear.'

May we all listen as children as we enter his garden.

Here is a selection, a bit of Blake, designed as a bedside companion or to accompany a walk in the countryside, to sit beneath a shady tree and discover a portal into his visionary and musical experience.

There is in his song something of the Appalachian, whose ballads immigrated from British soil. Threnody played with a dark fiddle. They remind me that when I was young I thought Blake was American. Many might claim him now.

Although much of his work seems impenetrable he never ceased in his desire to connect with the populace. He has succeeded in offering both. He has been the spiritual ancestor of generations of poets and alchemical detectives seeking their way through the labyrinth of inhuman knowledge even as schoolchildren recite his verses. His proverbs have become common parlance.

Passages of prophecy have been chosen as a lure, in appreciation of his rich language without the mystical fetters of a difficult cosmology. Fragments of his letters give us a glimpse into the poles of his daily existence, the ecstatic bursts, the trials of laborious poverty.

To take on Blake is not to be alone.

Walk with him. William Blake writes 'all is holy.'

That includes the book you are holding and the hand that holds it.

Patti Smith, 2007

POEMS

Trembling I sit day and night, my friends are astonish'd at me,
Yet they forgive my wanderings. I rest not from my great task!
To open the Eternal Worlds, to open the immortal Eyes
Of Man inwards into the Worlds of Thought, into Eternity
Ever expanding in the Bosom of God, the Human Imagination.
O Saviour pour upon me thy Spirit of meekness & love:
Annihilate the Selfhood in me: be thou all my life!
Guide thou my hand, which trembles exceedingly upon the rock
    of ages.

William Blake, Jerusalem

FROM *POETICAL SKETCHES*

TO THE
EVENING STAR

Thou fair-hair'd angel of the evening,
Now, whilst the sun rests on the mountains, light
Thy bright torch of love; thy radiant crown
Put on, and smile upon our evening bed!
Smile on our loves, and while thou drawest the
Blue curtains of the sky, scatter thy silver dew
On every flower that shuts its sweet eyes
In timely sleep. Let thy west wind sleep on
The lake; speak silence with thy glimmering eyes,
And wash the dusk with silver. Soon, full soon,
Dost thou withdraw; then the wolf rages wide,
And the lion glares thro' the dun forest:
The fleeces of our flocks are cover'd with
Thy sacred dew: protect them with thine influence.

TO SPRING

O thou, with dewy locks, who lookest down
Thro' the clear windows of the morning, turn
Thine angel eyes upon our western isle,
Which in full choir hails thy approach, O Spring!

The hills tell each other, and the list'ning
Vallies hear; all our longing eyes are turned
Up to thy bright pavilions: issue forth,
And let thy holy feet visit our clime.

Come o'er the eastern hills, and let our winds
Kiss thy perfumed garments; let us taste
Thy morn and evening breath; scatter thy pearls
Upon our love-sick land that mourns for thee.

O deck her forth with thy fair fingers; pour
Thy soft kisses on her bosom; and put
Thy golden crown upon her languish'd head,
Whose modest tresses were bound up for thee!

TO SUMMER

O thou who passest thro' our vallies in
Thy strength, curb thy fierce steeds, allay the heat
That flames from their large nostrils! thou, O Summer,
Oft pitched'st here thy golden tent, and oft
Beneath our oaks hast slept, while we beheld
With joy thy ruddy limbs and flourishing hair.

Beneath our thickest shades we oft have heard
Thy voice, when noon upon his fervid car
Rode o'er the deep of heaven; beside our springs
Sit down, and in our mossy valleys, on
Some bank beside a river clear, throw thy
Silk draperies off, and rush into the stream:
Our vallies love the Summer in his pride.

Our bards are fam'd who strike the silver wire:
Our youth are bolder than the southern swains:
Our maidens fairer in the sprightly dance:
We lack not songs, nor instruments of joy,
Nor echoes sweet, nor waters clear as heaven,
Nor laurel wreaths against the sultry heat.

TO AUTUMN

O Autumn, laden with fruit, and stained
With the blood of the grape, pass not, but sit
Beneath my shady roof; there thou may'st rest,
And tune thy jolly voice to my fresh pipe,
And all the daughters of the year shall dance!
Sing now the lusty song of fruits and flowers.

'The narrow bud opens her beauties to
The sun, and love runs in her thrilling veins;
Blossoms hang round the brows of morning, and
Flourish down the bright cheek of modest eve,
Till clust'ring Summer breaks forth into singing,
And feather'd clouds strew flowers round her head.

'The spirits of the air live on the smells
Of fruit; and joy, with pinions light, roves round
The gardens, or sits singing in the trees.'
Thus sang the jolly Autumn as he sat;
Then rose, girded himself, and o'er the bleak
Hills fled from our sight; but left his golden load.

TO WINTER

'O Winter! bar thine adamantine doors:
The north is thine; there hast thou built thy dark
Deep-founded habitation. Shake not thy roofs,
Nor bend thy pillars with thine iron car.'

He hears me not, but o'er the yawning deep
Rides heavy; his storms are unchain'd, sheathed
In ribbed steel; I dare not lift mine eyes,
For he hath rear'd his sceptre o'er the world.

Lo! now the direful monster, whose skin clings
To his strong bones, strides o'er the groaning rocks:
He withers all in silence, and his hand
Unclothes the earth, and freezes up frail life.

He takes his seat upon the cliffs; the mariner
Cries in vain. Poor little wretch! that deal'st
With storms; till heaven smiles, and the monster
Is driv'n yelling to his caves beneath mount Hecla.

TO MORNING

O holy virgin! clad in purest white,
Unlock heav'n's golden gates, and issue forth;
Awake the dawn that sleeps in heaven; let light
Rise from the chambers of the east, and bring
The honied dew that cometh on waking day.
O radiant morning, salute the sun
Rous'd like a huntsman to the chace, and with
Thy buskin'd feet appear upon our hills.

SONG

How sweet I roam'd from field to field
   And tasted all the summer's pride,
Till I the prince of love beheld
   Who in the sunny beams did glide!

He shew'd me lilies for my hair,
   And blushing roses for my brow;
He led me through his gardens fair
   Where all his golden pleasures grow.

With sweet May dews my wings were wet,
   And Phœbus fir'd my vocal rage;
He caught me in his silken net,
   And shut me in his golden cage.

He loves to sit and hear me sing,
   Then, laughing, sports and plays with me;
Then stretches out my golden wing,
   And mocks my loss of liberty.

SONG

My silks and fine array,
   My smiles and languish'd air,
By love are driv'n away;
   And mournful lean Despair
Brings me yew to deck my grave;
Such end true lovers have.

His face is fair as heav'n
   When springing buds unfold;
O why to him was't giv'n
   Whose heart is wintry cold?
His breast is love's all worship'd tomb,
Where all love's pilgrims come.

Bring me an axe and spade,
   Bring me a winding sheet;
When I my grave have made
   Let winds and tempests beat:
Then down I'll lie, as cold as clay.
True love doth pass away!

MAD SONG

The wild winds weep,
   And the night is a-cold;
Come hither, Sleep,
   And my griefs unfold:
But lo! the morning peeps
   Over the eastern steeps,
And the rustling birds of dawn
The earth do scorn.

Lo! to the vault
   Of paved heaven,
With sorrow fraught
   My notes are driven:
They strike the ear of night,
   Make weep the eyes of day;
They make mad the roaring winds,
   And with tempests play.

Like a fiend in a cloud
   With howling woe,
After night I do croud,
   And with night will go;
I turn my back to the east
From whence comforts have increas'd;
For light doth seize my brain
With frantic pain.

TO THE MUSES

Whether on Ida's shady brow,
Or in the chambers of the East,
The chambers of the sun, that now
From antient melody have ceas'd;

Whether in Heav'n ye wander fair,
Or the green corners of the earth,
Or the blue regions of the air
Where the melodious winds have birth;

Whether on chrystal rocks ye rove,
Beneath the bosom of the sea
Wand'ring in many a coral grove,
Fair Nine, forsaking Poetry!

How have you left the antient love
That bards of old enjoy'd in you!
The languid strings do scarcely move!
The sound is forc'd, the notes are few!

SONG

Fresh from the dewy hill, the merry year
Smiles on my head and mounts his flaming car;
Round my young brows the laurel wreathes a shade,
And rising glories beam around my head.

My feet are wing'd, while o'er the dewy lawn,
I meet my maiden risen like the morn:
O bless those holy feet, like angels' feet;
O bless those limbs, beaming with heav'nly light!

Like as an angel glitt'ring in the sky
In times of innocence and holy joy;
The joyful shepherd stops his grateful song
To hear the music of an angel's tongue.

So when she speaks, the voice of Heaven I hear;
So when we walk, nothing impure comes near;
Each field seems Eden, and each calm retreat;
Each village seems the haunt of holy feet.

But that sweet village where my black-ey'd maid
Closes her eyes in sleep beneath night's shade,
Whene'er I enter, more than mortal fire
Burns in my soul, and does my song inspire.

SONG

Memory, hither come,
    And tune your merry notes;
And, while upon the wind
    Your music floats,
I'll pore upon the stream
Where sighing lovers dream,
And fish for fancies as they pass
Within the watery glass.

I'll drink of the clear stream,
    And hear the linnet's song;
And there I'll lie and dream
    The day along:
And when night comes, I'll go
    To places fit for woe,
Walking along the darken'd valley
    With silent Melancholy.

from KING EDWARD THE THIRD

SCENE. *The Coast of France.* KING EDWARD *and Nobles before it. The Army.*

KING. O thou, to whose fury the nations are
But as dust! maintain thy servant's right.
Without thine aid, the twisted mail, and spear,
And forged helm, and shield of seven times beaten brass,
Are idle trophies of the vanquisher.
When confusion rages, when the field is in a flame,
When the cries of blood tear horror from heav'n,
And yelling death runs up and down the ranks,
Let Liberty, the charter'd right of Englishmen,
Won by our fathers in many a glorious field,
Enerve my soldiers; let Liberty
Blaze in each countenance, and fire the battle.
The enemy fight in chains, invisible chains, but heavy;
Their minds are fetter'd, then how can they be free?
While, like the mounting flame,
We spring to battle o'er the floods of death,
And these fair youths, the flow'r of England,
Vent'ring their lives in my most righteous cause,
O sheathe their hearts with triple steel, that they
May emulate their fathers' virtues!
And thou, my son, be strong; thou fightest for a crown
That death can never ravish from thy brow,
A crown of glory: but from thy very dust
Shall beam a radiance, to fire the breasts
Of youth unborn! Our names are written equal
In fame's wide trophied hall; 'tis ours to gild
The letters, and to make them shine with gold
That never tarnishes: whether Third Edward,
Or the Prince of Wales, or Montacute, or Mortimer,
Or ev'n the least by birth, shall gain the brightest fame,
Is in his hand to whom all men are equal.

The world of men are like the num'rous stars
That beam and twinkle in the depth of night,
Each clad in glory according to his sphere;
But we, that wander from our native seats
And beam forth lustre on a darkling world,
Grow larger as we advance! and some perhaps
The most obscure at home, that scarce were seen
To twinkle in their sphere, may so advance
That the astonish'd world, with up-turn'd eyes,
Regardless of the moon, and those that once were bright,
Stand only for to gaze upon their splendour!

       [He here knights the Prince, and other young Nobles.]
Now let us take a just revenge for those
Brave Lords, who fell beneath the bloody axe
At Paris. Thanks, noble Harcourt, for 'twas
By your advice we landed here in Brittany,
A country not yet sown with destruction,
And where the fiery whirlwind of swift war
Has not yet swept its desolating wing.—
Into three parties we divide by day,
And separate march, but join again at night;
Each knows his rank, and Heav'n marshal all.   *[Exeunt.*

★   ★   ★

SCENE. *In the Camp. Several of the Warriors met at the King's Tent with a Minstrel, who sings the following Song:*

O Sons of Trojan Brutus, cloath'd in war,
Whose voices are the thunder of the field,
Rolling dark clouds o'er France, muffling the sun
In sickly darkness like a dim eclipse,
Threatening as the red brow of storms, as fire
Burning up nations in your wrath and fury!

Your ancestors came from the fires of Troy,
(Like lions rouz'd by light'ning from their dens,
Whose eyes do glare against the stormy fires)
Heated with war, fill'd with the blood of Greeks,
With helmets hewn, and shields covered with gore,
In navies black, broken with wind and tide!

They landed in firm array upon the rocks
Of Albion; they kiss'd the rocky shore;
'Be thou our mother and our nurse,' they said;
'Our children's mother, and thou shalt be our grave,
The sepulchre of ancient Troy, from whence
Shall rise cities, and thrones, and arms, and awful pow'rs.'

Our fathers swarm from the ships. Giant voices
Are heard from the hills, the enormous sons
Of Ocean run from rocks and caves: wild men,
Naked and roaring like lions, hurling rocks,
And wielding knotty clubs, like oaks entangled
Thick as a forest, ready for the axe.

Our fathers move in firm array to battle;
The savage monsters rush like roaring fire;
Like as a forest roars with crackling flames,
When the red lightning, borne by furious storms,
Lights on some woody shore; the parched heavens
Rain fire into the molten raging sea!

The smoaking trees are strewn upon the shore,
Spoil'd of their verdure! O how oft have they
Defy'd the storm that howled o'er their heads!
Our fathers, sweating, lean on their spears, and view
The mighty dead: giant bodies streaming blood,
Dread visages frowning in silent death!

Then Brutus spoke, inspir'd; our fathers sit
Attentive on the melancholy shore:
Hear ye the voice of Brutus—'The flowing waves
Of time come rolling o'er my breast,' he said;
'And my heart labours with futurity:
Our sons shall rule the empire of the sea.

'Their mighty wings shall stretch from east to west.
Their nest is in the sea, but they shall roam
Like eagles for the prey; nor shall the young
Crave or be heard; for plenty shall bring forth,
Cities shall sing, and vales in rich array
Shall laugh, whose fruitful laps bend down with fulness.

'Our sons shall rise from thrones in joy,
Each one buckling on his armour; Morning
Shall be prevented by their swords gleaming,
And Evening hear their song of victory!
Their towers shall be built upon the rocks,
Their daughters shall sing, surrounded with shining spears!

'Liberty shall stand upon the cliffs of Albion,
Casting her blue eyes over the green ocean;
Or, tow'ring, stand upon the roaring waves,
Stretching her mighty spear o'er distant lands;
While, with her eagle wings, she covereth
Fair Albion's shore, and all her families.'

PROLOGUE

KING EDWARD THE FOURTH

O for a voice like thunder, and a tongue
To drown the throat of war! When the senses
Are shaken, and the soul is driven to madness,
Who can stand? When the souls of the oppressed
Fight in the troubled air that rages, who can stand?
When the whirlwind of fury comes from the
Throne of God, when the frowns of his countenance
Drive the nations together, who can stand?
When Sin claps his broad wings over the battle,
And sails rejoicing in the flood of Death;
When souls are torn to everlasting fire,
And fiends of Hell rejoice upon the slain,
O who can stand? O who hath caused this?
O who can answer at the throne of God?
The Kings and Nobles of the Land have done it!
Hear it not, Heaven, thy Ministers have done it!

PROLOGUE TO KING JOHN

Justice hath heaved a sword to plunge in Albion's breast; for Albion's sins are crimson dy'd, and the red scourge follows her desolate sons! Then Patriot rose; full oft did Patriot rise, when Tyranny hath stain'd fair Albion's breast with her own children's gore. Round his majestic feet deep thunders roll; each heart does tremble, and each knee grows slack. The stars of heaven tremble; the roaring voice of war, the trumpet, calls to battle! Brother in brother's blood must bathe, rivers of death! O land, most hapless! O beauteous island, how forsaken! Weep from thy silver fountains; weep from thy gentle rivers! The angel of the island weeps! Thy widowed virgins weep beneath thy shades! Thy aged fathers gird themselves for war! The sucking infant lives to die in battle; the weeping mother feeds him for the slaughter! The husbandman doth leave his bending harvest! Blood cries afar! The land doth sow itself! The glittering youth of courts must gleam in arms! The aged senators their ancient swords assume! The trembling sinews of old age must work the work of death against their progeny; for Tyranny hath stretch'd his purple arm, and 'blood,' he cries; 'the chariots and the horses, the noise of shout, and dreadful thunder of the battle heard afar!' Beware, O Proud! thou shalt be humbled; thy cruel brow, thine iron heart, is smitten, though lingering Fate is slow. O yet may Albion smile again, and stretch her peaceful arms, and raise her golden head exultingly! Her citizens shall throng about her gates, her mariners shall sing upon the sea, and myriads shall to her temples crowd! Her sons shall joy as in the morning! Her daughters sing as to the rising year!

A WAR SONG TO
ENGLISHMEN

Prepare, prepare the iron helm of war,
Bring forth the lots, cast in the spacious orb;
Th' Angel of Fate turns them with mighty hands
And casts them out upon the darken'd earth!
                              Prepare, prepare.

Prepare your hearts for Death's cold hand! prepare
Your souls for flight, your bodies for the earth!
Prepare your arms for glorious victory!
Prepare your eyes to meet a holy God!
                              Prepare, prepare.

Whose fatal scroll is that? Methinks 'tis mine!
Why sinks my heart, why faultereth my tongue?
Had I three lives, I'd die in such a cause,
And rise, with ghosts, over the well-fought field.
                              Prepare, prepare.

The arrows of Almighty God are drawn!
Angels of Death stand in the low'ring heavens!
Thousands of souls must seek the realms of light,
And walk together on the clouds of heaven!
                              Prepare, prepare.

Soldiers, prepare! Our cause is Heaven's cause;
Soldiers, prepare! Be worthy of our cause:
Prepare to meet our fathers in the sky:
Prepare, O troops, that are to fall to-day!
                              Prepare, prepare.

Alfred shall smile, and make his harp rejoice;
The Norman William, and the learned Clerk,
And Lion Heart, and black-brow'd Edward, with
His loyal queen, shall rise, and welcome us!
                              Prepare, prepare.

THE COUCH OF DEATH

The veiled Evening walked solitary down the western hills, and Silence reposed in the valley; the birds of day were heard in their nests, rustling in brakes and thickets; and the owl and bat flew round the darkening trees: all is silent when Nature takes her repose.—In former times, on such an evening, when the cold clay breathed with life, and our ancestors, who now sleep in their graves, walked on the stedfast globe, the remains of a family of the tribes of Earth, a mother and a sister, were gathered to the sick bed of a youth. Sorrow linked them together, leaning on one another's necks alternately—like lilies, dropping tears in each other's bosom, they stood by the bed like reeds bending over a lake, when the evening drops trickle down. His voice was low as the whisperings of the woods when the wind is asleep, and the visions of Heaven unfold their visitation. 'Parting is hard and death is terrible; I seem to walk through a deep valley, far from the light of day, alone and comfortless! The damps of death fall thick upon me! Horrors stare me in the face! I look behind, there is no returning; Death follows after me; I walk in regions of Death, where no tree is, without a lantern to direct my steps, without a staff to support me.' Thus he laments through the still evening, till the curtains of darkness were drawn. Like the sound of a broken pipe, the aged woman raised her voice. 'O my son, my son, I know but little of the path thou goest! But lo! there is a God, who made the world; stretch out thy hand to Him.' The youth replied, like a voice heard from a sepulchre, 'My hand is feeble, how should I stretch it out? My ways are sinful, how should I raise mine eyes? My voice hath used deceit, how should I call on Him who is Truth? My breath is loathsome, how should he not be offended? If I lay my face in the dust, the grave opens its mouth for me; if I lift up my head, sin covers me as a cloak! O my dear friends, pray ye for me! Stretch forth your hands that my helper may come! Through the void space I walk, between the sinful world and eternity! Beneath me burns eternal fire! O for a hand to pluck me forth!' As the voice of an omen heard in the silent valley, when the few inhabitants cling trembling together; as the voice of the Angel of Death, when the thin beams of the moon give a faint light, such was this young man's voice to his friends! Like the bubbling waters of the brook in the dead of night, the aged woman raised her cry, and said, 'O Voice, that dwellest in my breast, can I not cry, and lift my eyes to Heaven? Thinking of this, my spirit is turned within me into confusion! O my child, my child! is thy breath infected? So is mine. As the deer, wounded by the brooks of water, so the arrows of sin stick in my flesh; the poison hath entered into my marrow.' Like rolling waves upon a desert shore, sighs succeeded sighs; they covered their faces and wept! The youth lay silent, his mother's arm was under his head; he was like a cloud tossed by the winds, till the sun shine, and the drops of rain glisten, the yellow harvest breathes, and the thankful eyes of the villagers are turned up in smiles. The traveller that hath taken shelter under an oak, eyes the distant country with joy! Such smiles were seen upon the face of the youth! a visionary hand wiped away his tears, and a ray of light beamed around his head! All was still. The moon hung not out her lamp, and the stars faintly glimmered in the summer sky; the breath of night slept among the leaves of the forest; the bosom of the lofty hill drank in the silent dew, while on his majestic brow the voice of Angels is heard, and stringed sounds ride upon the wings of night. The sorrowful pair lift up their heads, hovering Angels are around them, voices of comfort are heard over the Couch of Death, and the youth breathes out his soul with joy into eternity.

CONTEMPLATION

Who is this, that with unerring step dares tempt the wilds, where only Nature's foot hath trod? 'Tis Contemplation, daughter of the grey Morning! Majestical she steppeth, and with her pure quill on every flower writeth Wisdom's name. Now lowly bending, whispers in mine ear, 'O man, how great, how little thou! O man, slave of each moment, lord of eternity! seest thou where Mirth sits on the painted cheek? doth it not seem ashamed of such a place, and grow immoderate to brave it out? O what an humble garb true Joy puts on! Those who want Happiness must stoop to find it; it is a flower that grows in every vale. Vain foolish man, that roams on lofty rocks! where, 'cause his garments are swoln with wind, he fancies he is grown into a giant! Lo, then, Humility, take it, and wear it in thine heart; lord of thyself, thou then art lord of all. Clamour brawls along the streets, and destruction hovers in the city's smoak; but on these plains, and in these silent woods, true joys descend: here build thy nest; here fix thy staff; delights blossom around; numberless beauties blow; the green grass springs in joy, and the nimble air kisses the leaves; the brook stretches its arms along the velvet meadow, its silver inhabitants sport and play; the youthful sun joys like a hunter roused to the chace: he rushes up the sky, and lays hold on the immortal coursers of day; the sky glitters with the jingling trappings! Like a triumph, season follows season, while the airy music fills the world with joyful sounds.' I answered, 'Heavenly goddess! I am wrapped in mortality, my flesh is a prison, my bones the bars of death, Misery builds over our cottage roofs, and Discontent runs like a brook. Even in childhood, Sorrow slept with me in my cradle; he followed me up and down in the house when I grew up; he was my school-fellow: thus he was in my steps and in my play, till he became to me as my brother. I walked through dreary places with him, and in church-yards; and I oft found myself sitting by Sorrow on a tomb-stone!'

FROM THE PICKERING
MANUSCRIPT

The Smile

There is a Smile of Love,
And there is a Smile of Deceit,
And there is a Smile of Smiles
In which these two Smiles meet,

And there is a Frown of Hate,
And there is a Frown of Disdain,
And there is a Frown of Frowns
Which you strive to forget in vain;

For it sticks in the Heart's deep Core
And it sticks in the deep Back bone,
And no Smile that ever was smil'd,
But only one Smile alone,

That betwixt the Cradle & Grave
It only once Smil'd can be;
But, when it once is Smil'd,
There's an end to all Misery.

The Golden Net

Three Virgins at the break of day:
'Whither, young Man, whither away?
Alas for woe! alas for woe!'
They cry, & tears for ever flow.
The one was Cloth'd in flames of fire,
The other Cloth'd in iron wire,
The other Cloth'd in tears & sighs.
Dazling bright before my Eyes
They bore a Net of golden twine
To hang upon the Branches fine.
Pitying I wept to see the woe
That Love & Beauty undergo,
To be consum'd in burning Fires
And in ungratified Desires,
And in tears cloth'd night & day
Melted all my Soul away.
When they saw my Tears, a Smile
That did Heaven itself beguile,
Bore the Golden Net aloft
As on downy Pinions soft
Over the Morning of my Day.
Underneath the Net I stray,
Now intreating Burning Fire,
Now intreating Iron Wire,
Now intreating Tears & Sighs,
O when will the morning rise?

The Mental Traveller

I travel'd thro' a Land of Men,
A Land of Men & Women too,
And heard & saw such dreadful things
As cold Earth wanderers never knew.

For there the Babe is born in joy
That was begotten in dire woe,
Just as we Reap in joy the fruit
Which we in bitter tears did sow.

And if the Babe is born a Boy
He's given to a Woman Old
Who nails him down upon a rock,
Catches his shrieks in cups of gold.

She binds iron thorns around his head,
She pierces both his hands & feet,
She cuts his heart out at his side
To make it feel both cold & heat.

Her fingers number every Nerve,
Just as a Miser counts his gold;
She lives upon his shrieks & cries,
And She grows young as he grows old.

Till he becomes a bleeding youth
And She becomes a Virgin bright;
Then he rends up his Manacles
And binds her down for his delight.

He plants himself in all her Nerves,
Just as a Husbandman his mould;
And She becomes his dwelling place
And Garden fruitful seventy fold.

An Aged Shadow, soon he fades,
Wand'ring round an Earthly Cot,
Full filled all with gems & gold
Which he by industry had got.

And these are the gems of the Human Soul,
The rubies & pearls of a lovesick eye,
The countless gold of the akeing heart,
The martyr's groan & the lover's sigh.

They are his meat, they are his drink;
He feeds the Beggar & the Poor
And the wayfaring Traveller:
For ever open is his door.

His grief is their eternal joy;
They make the roofs & walls to ring;
Till from the fire on the hearth
A little Female Babe does spring.

And She is all of solid fire
And gems & gold, that none his hand
Dares stretch to touch her Baby form,
Or wrap her in his swaddling-band.

But She comes to the Man she loves,
If young or old, or rich or poor;
They soon drive out the aged Host,
A Beggar at another's door,

He wanders weeping far away,
Untill some other take him in;
Oft blind & age-bent, sore distrest,
Untill he can a Maiden win.

And to allay his freezing Age,
The Poor Man takes her in his arms;
The Cottage fades before his sight,
The Garden & its lovely Charms.

The Guests are scatter'd thro' the land,
For the Eye altering alters all;
The Senses roll themselves in fear
And the flat Earth becomes a Ball;

The Stars, Sun, Moon, all shrink away,
A desart vast without a bound,
And nothing left to eat or drink,
And a dark desart all around.

The honey of her Infant lips,
The bread & wine of her sweet smile,
The wild game of her roving eye,
Does him to Infancy beguile;

For as he eats & drinks he grows
Younger & younger every day;
And on the desart wild they both
Wander in terror & dismay.

Like the wild Stag she flees away,
Her fear plants many a thicket wild;
While he pursues her night & day,
By various arts of Love beguil'd;

By various arts of Love & Hate,
Till the wide desart planted o'er
With Labyrinths of wayward Love,
Where roams the Lion, Wolf & Boar;

Till he becomes a wayward Babe,
And she a weeping Woman Old;
Then many a Lover wanders here,
The Sun & Stars are nearer roll'd,

The trees bring forth sweet Extacy
To all who in the desart roam,
Till many a City there is Built
And many a pleasant Shepherd's home

But when they find the frowning Babe,
Terror strikes thro' the region wide:
They cry, 'the Babe! the Babe is Born!'
And flee away on every side.

For who dare touch the frowning form,
His arm is wither'd to its root;
Lions, Boars, Wolves, all howling flee,
And every Tree does shed its fruit.

And none can touch that frowning form,
Except it be a Woman Old;
She nails him down upon the Rock,
And all is done as I have told.

The Land of Dreams

'Awake, awake, my little Boy!
Thou wast thy Mother's only joy;
Why dost thou weep in thy gentle sleep?
Awake! thy Father does thee keep.'

'O what Land is the Land of Dreams?
What are its Mountains, & what are its Streams?
O Father! I saw my Mother there,
Among the Lillies by waters fair.

'Among the Lambs, clothed in white,
She walk'd with her Thomas in sweet delight.
I wept for joy, like a dove I mourn;
O when shall I again return?'

'Dear Child, I also by pleasant Streams
Have wander'd all Night in the Land of Dreams;
But tho' calm & warm the waters wide,
I could not get to the other side.'

'Father, O father! what do we here
In this Land of unbelief & fear?
The Land of Dreams is better far,
Above the light of the Morning Star.'

Mary

Sweet Mary, the first time she ever was there,
Came into the Ball room among the Fair;
The young Men & Maidens around her throng,
And these are the words upon every tongue:

'An Angel is here from the heavenly climes,
Or again does return the golden times;
Her eyes outshine every brilliant ray,
She opens her lips—'tis the Month of May.'

Mary moves in soft beauty & conscious delight,
To augment with sweet smiles all the joys of the Night,
Nor once blushes to own to the rest of the Fair
That sweet Love & Beauty are worthy our care.

In the Morning the Villagers rose with delight,
And repeated with pleasure the joys of the night,
And Mary arose among Friends to be free,
But no Friend from henceforward thou, Mary, shalt see.

Some said she was proud, some call'd her a whore,
And some, when she passed by, shut to the door;
A damp cold came o'er her, her blushes all fled;
Her lillies & roses are blighted & shed.

'O why was I born with a different Face?
Why was I not born like this Envious Race?
Why did Heaven adorn me with bountiful hand,
And then set me down in an envious Land?

'To be weak as a Lamb & smooth as a Dove,
And not to raise Envy, is call'd Christian Love;
But if you raise Envy your Merit's to blame
For planting such spite in the weak & the tame.

'I will humble my Beauty, I will not dress fine,
I will keep from the Ball, & my Eyes shall not shine;
And if any Girl's Lover forsakes her for me
I'll refuse him my hand, & from Envy be free.'

She went out in Morning, attir'd plain & neat;
'Proud Mary's gone Mad,' said the Child in the Street;
She went out in Morning in plain neat attire,
And came home in Evening bespatter'd with mire.

She trembled & wept, sitting on the Bed side,
She forgot it was Night, & she trembled & cried;
She forgot it was Night, she forgot it was Morn,
Her soft Memory imprinted with Faces of Scorn;

With Faces of Scorn & with Eyes of Disdain
Like foul Fiends inhabiting Mary's mild Brain,
She remembers no Face like the Human Divine;
All Faces have Envy, sweet Mary, but thine;

And thine is a Face of sweet Love in despair,
And thine is a Face of mild sorrow & care,
And thine is a Face of wild terror & fear
That shall never be quiet till laid on its bier.

The Crystal Cabinet

The Maiden caught me in the Wild,
Where I was dancing merrily;
She put me into her Cabinet,
And Lock'd me up with a golden Key.

This Cabinet is form'd of Gold
And Pearl & Crystal shining bright,
And within it opens into a World
And a little lovely Moony Night.

Another England there I saw,
Another London with its Tower,
Another Thames & other Hills,
And another pleasant Surrey Bower,

Another Maiden like herself,
Translucent, lovely, shining clear,
Threefold each in the other clos'd—
O what a pleasant trembling fear!

O what a smile! a threefold Smile
Fill'd me, that like a flame I burn'd;
I bent to Kiss the lovely Maid,
And found a Threefold Kiss return'd.

I strove to sieze the inmost Form
With ardor fierce & hands of flame,
But burst the Crystal Cabinet
And like a Weeping Babe became:

A weeping Babe upon the wild,
And weeping Woman pale reclin'd,
And in the outward air again
I fill'd with woes the passing Wind.

Auguries of Innocence

To see a World in a Grain of Sand
And a Heaven in a Wild Flower,
Hold Infinity in the palm of your hand
And Eternity in an hour.

A Robin Red breast in a Cage
Puts all Heaven in a Rage.

A Dove house fill'd with Doves & Pigeons
Shudders Hell thro' all its regions.

A Dog starv'd at his Master's Gate
Predicts the ruin of the State.

A Horse misus'd upon the Road
Calls to Heaven for Human blood.

Each outcry of the hunted Hare
A fibre from the Brain does tear.

A Skylark wounded in the wing,
A Cherubim does cease to sing.

The Game Cock clip'd & arm'd for fight
Does the Rising Sun affright.

Every Wolf's & Lion's howl
Raises from Hell a Human Soul.

The wild Deer wand'ring here & there
Keeps the Human Soul from Care.

The Lamb misus'd breeds Public strife
And yet forgives the Butcher's Knife.

The Bat that flits at close of Eve
Has left the Brain that won't Believe.
The Owl that calls upon the Night
Speaks the Unbeliever's fright.

He who shall hurt the little Wren
Shall never be belov'd by Men.

He who the Ox to wrath has mov'd
Shall never be by Woman lov'd.

The wanton Boy that kills the Fly
Shall feel the Spider's enmity.

He who torments the Chafer's sprite
Weaves a Bower in endless Night.

The Catterpiller on the Leaf
Repeats to thee thy Mother's grief.

Kill not the Moth nor Butterfly
For the Last Judgment draweth nigh.

He who shall train the Horse to war
Shall never pass the Polar Bar.

The Beggar's Dog & Widow's Cat,
Feed them, & thou wilt grow fat.

The Gnat that sings his Summer's song
Poison gets from Slander's tongue.
The poison of the Snake & Newt
Is the sweat of Envy's Foot.
The Poison of the Honey Bee
Is the Artist's Jealousy.

The Prince's Robes & Beggar's Rags
Are Toadstools on the Miser's Bags.

A truth that's told with bad intent
Beats all the Lies you can invent.
It is right it should be so;
Man was made for Joy & Woe,
And when this we rightly know,
Thro' the World we safely go.

Joy & Woe are woven fine,
A Clothing for the Soul divine;
Under every grief & pine
Runs a joy with silken twine.

The Babe is more than Swadling Bands,
Throughout all these Human Lands;
Tools were made, & Born were hands,
Every Farmer Understands.

Every Tear from Every Eye
Becomes a Babe in Eternity;
This is caught by Females bright
And return'd to its own delight.

The Bleat, the Bark, Bellow & Roar
Are Waves that Beat on Heaven's Shore.

The Babe that weeps the Rod beneath
Writes Revenge in realms of Death.

The Beggar's Rags fluttering in Air
Does to Rags the Heavens tear.

The Soldier arm'd with Sword & Gun
Palsied strikes the Summer's Sun.

The poor Man's Farthing is worth more
Than all the Gold on Afric's Shore.

One Mite wrung from the Lab'rer's hands
Shall buy & sell the Miser's Lands
Or if protected from on high
Does that whole Nation sell & buy.

He who mocks the Infant's Faith
Shall be mock'd in Age & Death.
He who shall teach the Child to Doubt
The rotting Grave shall ne'er get out.
He who respects the Infant's faith
Triumphs over Hell & Death.

The Child's Toys & the Old Man's Reasons
Are the Fruits of the Two seasons.

The Questioner who sits so sly
Shall never know how to Reply.
He who replies to words of Doubt
Doth put the Light of Knowledge out.

The Strongest Poison ever known
Came from Cæsar's Laurel Crown.

Nought can deform the Human Race
Like to the Armour's iron brace.

When Gold & Gems adorn the Plow
To peaceful Arts shall Envy Bow.

A Riddle or the Cricket's Cry
Is to Doubt a fit Reply.

The Emmet's Inch & Eagle's Mile
Make Lame Philosophy to smile.

He who Doubts from what he sees
Will ne'er Believe, do what you Please.
If the Sun & Moon should doubt,
They'd immediately Go out.

To be in a Passion you Good may do,
But no Good if a Passion is in you.

The Whore & Gambler, by the State
Licenc'd, build that Nation's Fate.
The Harlot's cry from Street to Street
Shall weave Old England's winding Sheet.
The Winner's Shout, the Loser's Curse,
Dance before dead England's Hearse.

Every Night & every Morn
Some to Misery are Born.
Every Morn & every Night
Some are Born to sweet delight.
Some are Born to sweet delight,
Some are Born to Endless Night.

We are led to Believe a Lie
When we see not Thro' the Eye
Which was Born in a Night, to perish in a Night,
When the Soul Slept in Beams of Light.

God Appears, & God is Light
To those poor Souls who dwell in Night,
But does a Human Form Display
To those who Dwell in Realms of Day.

William Bond

I wonder whether the Girls are mad,
And I wonder whether they mean to kill,
And I wonder if William Bond will die,
For assuredly he is very ill.

He went to Church in a May morning,
Attended by Fairies, one, two, & three;
But the Angels of Providence drove them away,
And he return'd home in Misery.

He went not out to the Field nor Fold,
He went not out to the Village nor Town,
But he came home in a black black cloud,
And he took to his Bed, & there lay down.

And an Angel of Providence at his Feet,
And an Angel of Providence at his Head,
And in the midst a Black Black Cloud,
And in the midst the Sick Man on his Bed.

And on his Right hand was Mary Green,
And on his Left hand was his Sister Jane,
And their tears fell thro' the black black Cloud
To drive away the sick man's pain.

'O William, if thou dost another Love,
Dost another Love better than poor Mary,
Go & take that other to be thy Wife,
And Mary Green shall her Servant be.'

'Yes, Mary, I do another Love,
Another I love far better than thee,
And Another I will have for my Wife;
Then what have I to do with thee?

'For thou art Melancholy Pale,
And on thy Head is the cold Moon's Shine,
But she is ruddy & bright as day,
And the sun beams dazzle from her eyne.'

Mary trembled & Mary chill'd,
And Mary fell down on the right hand floor,
That William Bond & his Sister Jane
Scarce could recover Mary more.

When Mary woke & found her Laid
On the Right hand of her William dear,
On the Right hand of his loved Bed,
And saw her William Bond so near,

The Fairies that fled from William Bond
Danced around her Shining Head;
They danced over the Pillow white,
And the Angels of Providence left the Bed.

I thought Love liv'd in the hot sun shine,
But O he lives in the Moony light!
I thought to find Love in the heat of day,
But sweet Love is the Comforter of Night.

Seek Love in the Pity of others' Woe,
In the gentle relief of another's care,
In the darkness of night & the winter's snow,
In the naked & outcast, Seek Love there.

FROM BLAKE'S NOTEBOOK

The Birds

He. Where thou dwellest, in what grove,
    Tell me, Fair one, tell me love
    Where thou thy charming Nest doth build,
    O thou pride of every field!

She. Yonder stands a lonely tree,
    There I live & mourn for thee:
    Morning drinks my silent tear,
    And evening winds my sorrows bear.

He. O thou Summer's harmony,
    I have liv'd & mourn'd for thee:
    Each day I mourn along the wood,
    And night hath heard my sorrows loud.

She. Dost thou truly long for me?
    And am I thus sweet to thee?
    Sorrow now is at an End,
    O My Lover & my Friend!

He. Come, on wings of joy we'll fly
    To where my Bower hangs on high;
    Come & make thy calm retreat
    Among green leaves & blossoms sweet.

FROM *THE MARRIAGE OF HEAVEN AND HELL*

A Memorable Fancy

As I was walking among the fires of hell, delighted with the enjoyments of Genius, which to Angels look like torment and insanity, I collected some of their Proverbs, thinking that as the sayings used in a nation mark its character, so the Proverbs of Hell shew the nature of Infernal wisdom better than any description of buildings or garments.

When I came home, on the abyss of the five senses, where a flat sided steep frowns over the present world, I saw a mighty Devil folded in black clouds hovering on the sides of the rock: with corroding fires he wrote the following sentence now percieved by the minds of men, & read by them on earth.

How do you know but ev'ry Bird that cuts the airy way,
Is an immense world of delight, clos'd by your senses five?

from Proverbs of Hell

In seed time learn, in harvest teach, in winter enjoy.
Drive your cart and your plow over the bones of the dead.
The road of excess leads to the palace of wisdom.
Prudence is a rich ugly old maid courted by Incapacity.
He who desires but acts not, breeds pestilence.
The cut worm forgives the plow.
Dip him in the river who loves water.
A fool sees not the same tree that a wise man sees.
He whose face gives no light, shall never become a star.
Eternity is in love with the productions of time.
The busy bee has no time for sorrow.
The hours of folly are measur'd by the clock, but of wisdom no
clock can measure.
All wholsom food is caught without a net or a trap.
Bring out number weight & measure in a year of dearth.
No bird soars too high if he soars with his own wings.
A dead body revenges not injuries.
The most sublime act is to set another before you.
If the fool would persist in his folly he would become wise.
Folly is the cloke of knavery.
Shame is Pride's cloke.
Prisons are built with stones of Law, Brothels with bricks of
Religion.
The pride of the peacock is the glory of God.
The lust of the goat is the bounty of God.
The wrath of the lion is the wisdom of God.
The nakedness of woman is the work of God.
Excess of sorrow laughs. Excess of joy weeps.
The roaring of lions, the howling of wolves, the raging of the
stormy sea, and the destructive sword, are portions of eternity
too great for the eye of man.
The fox condemns the trap, not himself.
Joys impregnate. Sorrows bring forth.
Let man wear the fell of the lion, woman the fleece of the sheep.

The bird a nest, the spider a web, man friendship.

The selfish smiling fool, & the sullen frowning fool shall be both thought wise, that they may be a rod.

What is now proved was once only imagin'd.

The rat, the mouse, the fox, the rabbet, watch the roots; the lion, the tyger, the horse, the elephant, watch the fruits.

The cistern contains: the fountain overflows.

One thought fills immensity.

Always be ready to speak your mind and a base man will avoid you.

Every thing possible to be believ'd is an image of truth.

The eagle never lost so much time as when he submitted to learn of the crow.

The fox provides for himself, but God provides for the lion.

Think in the morning. Act in the noon. Eat in the evening. Sleep in the night.

He who has suffer'd you to impose on him knows you.

As the plow follows words, so God rewards prayers.

The tygers of wrath are wiser than the horses of instruction.

Expect poison from the standing water.

You never know what is enough unless you know what is more than enough.

Listen to the fool's reproach! it is a kingly title!

The eyes of fire, the nostrils of air, the mouth of water, the beard of earth.

The weak in courage is strong in cunning.

The apple tree never asks the beech how he shall grow, nor the lion the horse, how he shall take his prey.

The thankful reciever bears a plentiful harvest.

If others had not been foolish, we should be so.

The soul of sweet delight can never be defil'd.

When thou seest an Eagle, thou seest a portion of Genius, lift up thy head!

As the catterpiller chooses the fairest leaves to lay her eggs on, so the priest lays his curse on the fairest joys.

To create a little flower is the labour of ages.

Damn braces. Bless relaxes.

The best wine is the oldest, the best water the newest.
Prayers plow not! Praises reap not!
Joys laugh not! Sorrows weep not!

FROM *MILTON, A POEM IN 2 BOOKS*
To Justify the Ways of God to Men

from PREFACE

And did those feet in ancient time
Walk upon England's mountains green:
And was the holy Lamb of God
On England's pleasant pastures seen!

And did the Countenance Divine
Shine forth upon our clouded hills?
And was Jerusalem builded here
Among these dark Satanic Mills?

Bring me my Bow of burning gold:
Bring me my Arrows of desire:
Bring me my Spear: O clouds unfold!
Bring me my Chariot of fire!

I will not cease from Mental Fight,
Nor shall my Sword sleep in my hand
Till we have built Jerusalem
In England's green & pleasant Land.

Would to God that all the Lord's people were Prophets.

Numbers xi. Ch. 29 v.

from BOOK THE SECOND

There is a place where Contrarieties are equally True:
This place is called Beulah. It is a pleasant lovely Shadow
Where no dispute can come, Because of those who sleep.
Into this place the Sons & Daughters of Ololon descended
With solemn mourning, into Beulah's moony shades & hills
Weeping for Milton: mute wonder held the Daughters of Beulah,
Enraptur'd with affection sweet and mild benevolence.

Beulah is evermore Created around Eternity, appearing
To the Inhabitants of Eden around them on all sides.
But Beulah to its Inhabitants appears within each district
As the beloved infant in his mother's bosom round incircled
With arms of love & pity & sweet compassion. But to
The Sons of Eden the moony habitations of Beulah
Are from Great Eternity a mild & pleasant Rest.

And it is thus Created. Lo, the Eternal Great Humanity,
To whom be Glory & Dominion Evermore, Amen,
Walks among all his awful Family seen in every face:
As the breath of the Almighty, such are the words of man to man
In the great Wars of Eternity, in fury of Poetic Inspiration,
To build the Universe stupendous, Mental forms Creating.

But the Emanations trembled exceedingly, nor could they
Live, because the life of Man was too exceeding unbounded.
His joy became terrible to them; they trembled & wept,
Crying with one voice: 'Give us a habitation & a place
In which we may be hidden under the shadow of wings:
For if we, who are but for a time & who pass away in winter,

Behold these wonders of Eternity we shall consume:
But you, O our Fathers & Brothers, remain in Eternity.
But grant us a Temporal Habitation; do you speak
To us, we will obey your words as you obey Jesus
The Eternal who is blessed for ever & ever. Amen.'

So spake the lovely Emanations, & there appear'd a pleasant
Mild Shadow above, beneath, & on all sides round.

Into this pleasant Shadow all the weak & weary
Like Women & Children were taken away as on wings
Of dovelike softness, & shadowy habitations prepared for them.
But every Man return'd & went still going forward thro'
The Bosom of the Father in Eternity on Eternity,
Neither did any lack or fall into Error without
A Shadow to repose in all the Days of happy Eternity.

Into this pleasant Shadow, Beulah, all Ololon descended;
And when the Daughters of Beulah heard the lamentation
All Beulah wept, for they saw the Lord coming in the Clouds.
And the Shadows of Beulah terminate in rocky Albion.

And all Nations wept in affliction, Family by Family:
Germany wept towards France & Italy, England wept & trembled
Towards America, India rose up from his golden bed
As one awaken'd in the night; they saw the Lord coming
In the Clouds of Ololon with Power & Great Glory.

And all the Living Creatures of the Four Elements wail'd
With bitter wailing; these in the aggregate are named Satan
And Rahab: they know not of Regeneration, but only of Generation:
The Fairies, Nymphs, Gnomes & Genii of the Four Elements,
Unforgiving & unalterable, these cannot be Regenerated
But must be Created, for they know only of Generation:
These are the Gods of the Kingdoms of the Earth, in contrarious
And cruel opposition, Element against Element, opposed in War

Not Mental, as the Wars of Eternity, but a Corporeal Strife
In Los's Halls, continual labouring in the Furnaces of Golgonooza.
Orc howls on the Atlantic: Enitharmon trembles: All Beulah weeps.

Thou hearest the Nightingale begin the Song of Spring.
The Lark sitting upon his earthly bed, just as the morn
Appears, listens silent; then springing from the waving Corn-field,
    loud
He leads the Choir of Day: trill, trill, trill, trill,
Mounting upon the wings of light into the Great Expanse,
Reecchoing against the lovely blue & shining heavenly Shell,
His little throat labours with inspiration, every feather
On throat & breast & wings vibrates with the effluence Divine,
All Nature listens silent to him, & the awful Sun
Stands still upon the Mountain looking on this little Bird
With eyes of soft humility & wonder, love & awe.
Then loud from their green covert all the Birds begin their Song:
The Thrush, the Linnet & the Goldfinch, Robin & the Wren
Awake the Sun from his sweet reverie upon the Mountain.
The Nightingale again assays his song, & thro' the day
And thro' the night warbles luxuriant, every Bird of Song
Attending his loud harmony with admiration & love.
This is a vision of the lamentation of Beulah over Ololon.

Thou percievest the Flowers put forth their precious Odours,
And none can tell how from so small a center comes such sweets,
Forgetting that within that Center Eternity expands
Its ever during doors that Og & Anak fiercely guard.
First, e'er the morning breaks, joy opens in the flowery bosoms,
Joy even to tears, which the Sun rising dries: first the Wild Thyme
And Meadow-sweet, downy & soft, waving among the reeds,
Light springing on the air, lead the sweet Dance: they wake
The Honeysuckle sleeping on the Oak; the flaunting beauty
Revels along upon the wind; the White-thorn, lovely May,
Opens her many lovely eyes: listening the Rose still sleeps,
None dare to wake her; soon she bursts her crimson curtain'd bed

And comes forth in the majesty of beauty: every Flower,
The Pink, the Jessamine, the Wall-flower, the Carnation,
The Jonquil, the mild Lilly opes her heavens; every Tree
And Flower & Herb soon fill the air with an innumerable Dance,
Yet all in order sweet & lovely. Men are sick with Love.
Such is a Vision of the lamentation of Beulah over Ololon.

★   ★   ★

'To bathe in the Waters of Life, to wash off the Not Human,
I come in Self-annihilation & the grandeur of Inspiration,
To cast off Rational Demonstration by Faith in the Saviour,
To cast off the rotten rags of Memory by Inspiration,
To cast off Bacon, Locke & Newton from Albion's covering,
To take off his filthy garments & clothe him with Imagination;
To cast aside from Poetry all that is not Inspiration,
That it no longer shall dare to mock with the aspersion of
    Madness
Cast on the Inspired by the tame high finisher of paltry Blots
Indefinite, or paltry Rhymes, or paltry Harmonies,
Who creeps into State Government like a catterpiller to destroy;
To cast off the idiot Questioner who is always questioning
But never capable of answering, who sits with a sly grin
Silent plotting when to question, like a thief in a cave,
Who publishes doubt & calls it knowledge, whose Science is
    Despair,
Whose pretence to knowledge is Envy, whose whole Science is
To destroy the wisdom of ages to gratify ravenous Envy
That rages round him like a Wolf day & night without rest:
He smiles with condescension, he talks of Benevolence & Virtue,
And those who act with Benevolence & Virtue they murder time
    on time.
These are the destroyers of Jerusalem, these are the murderers
Of Jesus, who deny the Faith & mock at Eternal Life,
Who pretend to Poetry that they may destroy Imagination
By imitation of Nature's Images drawn from Remembrance.

These are the Sexual Garments, the Abomination of
   Desolation,
Hiding the Human Lineaments as with an Ark & Curtains
Which Jesus rent & now shall wholly purge away with Fire
Till Generation is swallow'd up in Regeneration.'

FROM *JERUSALEM*

from Chap: 3

'I gave thee liberty and life, O lovely Jerusalem,
And thou hast bound me down upon the Stems of Vegetation.
I gave thee Sheep-walks upon the Spanish Mountains, Jerusalem,
I gave thee Priam's City and the Isles of Grecia lovely,
I gave thee Hand & Scofield & the Counties of Albion,
They spread forth like a lovely root into the Garden of God,
They were as Adam before me, united into One Man,
They stood in innocence & their skiey tent reach'd over Asia
To Nimrod's Tower, to Ham & Canaan walking with Mizraim
Upon the Egyptian Nile, with solemn songs, to Grecia
And sweet Hesperia, even to Great Chaldea & Tesshina,
Following thee as a Shepherd by the Four Rivers of Eden.
Why wilt thou rend thyself apart, Jerusalem,
And build this Babylon, & sacrifice in secret Groves
Among the Gods of Asia, among the fountains of pitch & nitre?
Therefore thy Mountains are become barren, Jerusalem,
Thy Valleys, Plains of burning sand; thy Rivers, waters of death;
Thy Villages die of the Famine, and thy Cities
Beg bread from house to house, lovely Jerusalem.
Why wilt thou deface thy beauty & the beauty of thy little-ones
To please thy Idols in the pretended chastities of Uncircumcision?
Thy Sons are lovelier than Egypt or Assyria; wherefore
Dost thou blacken their beauty by a Secluded place of rest
And a peculiar Tabernacle, to cut the integuments of beauty
Into veils of tears and sorrows, O lovely Jerusalem?
They have perswaded thee to this; therefore their end shall come,
And I will lead thee thro' the Wilderness in shadow of my cloud,
And in my love I will lead thee, lovely Shadow of Sleeping Albion.'

This is the Song of the Lamb, sung by Slaves in evening time.

TO THE CHRISTIANS

Devils are
False Religions.
'Saul, Saul,
Why persecutest thou me?'

I give you the end of a golden string.
Only wind it into a ball,
It will lead you in at Heaven's gate
Built in Jerusalem's wall.

We are told to abstain from fleshly desires that we may lose no time from the Work of the Lord. Every moment lost is a moment that cannot be redeemed; every pleasure that intermingles with the duty of our station is a folly unredeemable, & is planted like the seed of a wild flower among our wheat. All the tortures of repentance are tortures of self-reproach on account of our leaving the Divine Harvest to the Enemy, the struggles of intanglement with incoherent roots. I know of no other Christianity and of no other Gospel than the liberty both of body & mind to exercise the Divine Arts of Imagination, Imagination, the real & eternal World of which this Vegetable Universe is but a faint shadow, & in which we shall live in our Eternal or Imaginative Bodies when these Vegetable Mortal Bodies are no more. The Apostles knew of no other Gospel. What were all their spiritual gifts? What is the Divine Spirit? is the Holy Ghost any other than an Intellectual Fountain? What is the Harvest of the Gospel & its Labours? What is that Talent which it is a curse to hide? What are the Treasures of Heaven which we are to lay up for ourselves, are they any other than Mental Studies & Performances? What are all the Gifts of the Gospel, are they not all Mental Gifts? Is God a Spirit who must be worshipped in Spirit & in Truth, and are not the Gifts of the Spirit Everything to Man? O ye Religious, discountenance every one among you who shall pretend to despise Art & Science! I call upon you in the Name of Jesus! What is the Life of Man but Art & Science? is it Meat & Drink? is not the Body more than Raiment? What is Mortality but the things relating to the Body which Dies? What is Immortality but the things relating to the Spirit which Lives Eternally? What is the Joy of Heaven but Improvement in the things of the Spirit? What are the Pains of Hell but Ignorance, Bodily Lust, Idleness & devastation of the things of the Spirit? Answer this to yourselves, & expel from among you those who pretend to despise the labours of Art & Science, which alone are the labours of the Gospel. Is not this plain & manifest to the thought? Can you think at all & not pronounce heartily That to Labour in Knowledge is to Build up Jerusalem, and to Despise Knowledge is to Despise Jerusalem & her Builders. And remember: He who despises & mocks a Mental Gift in another, calling it pride & selfishness & sin, mocks Jesus the giver of every Mental Gift, which always appear to the ignorance-loving Hypocrite as Sins; but that which is a Sin in the sight of cruel Man is not so in the sight of our kind God. Let every Christian, as much as in him lies, engage himself openly & publicly before all the World in some Mental pursuit for the Building up of Jerusalem.

I stood among my valleys of the south
And saw a flame of fire, even as a Wheel
Of fire surrounding all the heavens: it went
From west to east, against the current of
Creation, and devour'd all things in its loud
Fury & thundering course round heaven & earth.
By it the Sun was roll'd into an orb,
By it the Moon faded into a globe
Travelling thro' the night; for, from its dire
And restless fury, Man himself shrunk up
Into a little root a fathom long.
And I asked a Watcher & a Holy-One
Its Name; he answer'd: 'It is the Wheel of Religion.'
I wept & said: 'Is this the law of Jesus,
This terrible devouring sword turning every way?'
He answer'd: 'Jesus died because he strove

Against the current of this Wheel; its Name
Is Caiaphas, the dark Preacher of Death,
Of sin, of sorrow & of punishment:
Opposing Nature! It is Natural Religion;
But Jesus is the bright Preacher of Life
Creating Nature from this fiery Law
By self-denial & forgiveness of Sin.
Go therefore, cast out devils in Christ's name,
Heal thou the sick of spiritual disease,
Pity the evil, for thou art not sent
To smite with terror & with punishments
Those that are sick, like to the Pharisees
Crucifying & encompassing sea & land
For proselytes to tyranny & wrath;
But to the Publicans & Harlots go,
Teach them True Happiness, but let no curse
Go forth out of thy mouth to blight their peace;
For Hell is open'd to Heaven: thine eyes beheld
The dungeons burst & the Prisoners set free.'

 England! awake! awake! awake!
  Jerusalem thy Sister calls!
 Why wilt thou sleep the sleep of death?
  And close her from thy ancient walls.

 Thy hills & valleys felt her feet
  Gently upon their bosoms move:
 Thy gates beheld sweet Zion's ways:
  Then was a time of joy and love.

 And now the time returns again:
  Our souls exult, & London's towers
 Recieve the Lamb of God to dwell
  In England's green & pleasant bowers.

THE BOOK OF AHANIA

Chap: I[st]

1. Fuzon on a chariot iron-wing'd
On spiked flames rose: his hot visage
Flam'd furious; sparkles his hair & beard
Shot down his wide bosom and shoulders.
On clouds of smoke rages his chariot,
And his right hand burns red in its cloud,
Moulding into a vast globe his wrath
As the thunder-stone is moulded,
Son of Urizen's silent burnings.

2. 'Shall we worship this Demon of smoke,'
Said Fuzon, 'this abstract non-entity,
This cloudy God seated on waters,
Now seen, now obscur'd, King of Sorrow?'

3. So he spoke in a fiery flame,
On Urizen frowning indignant,
The Globe of wrath shaking on high.
Roaring with fury, he threw
The howling Globe; burning it flew,
Length'ning into a hungry beam. Swiftly

4. Oppos'd to the exulting flam'd beam
The broad Disk of Urizen upheav'd
Across the Void many a mile.

5. It was forg'd in mills where the winter
Beats incessant: ten winters the disk
Unremitting endur'd the cold hammer.

6. But the strong arm that sent it remember'd
The sounding beam: laughing, it tore through
That beaten mass, keeping its direction,
The cold loins of Urizen dividing.

7. Dire shriek'd his invisible Lust.
Deep groan'd Urizen! stretching his awful hand,
Ahania (so name his parted soul)
He siez'd on his mountains of Jealousy.
He groan'd, anguish'd, & called her Sin,
Kissing her and weeping over her;
Then hid her in darkness, in silence,
Jealous tho' she was invisible.

8. She fell down, a faint shadow wand'ring
In chaos and circling dark Urizen
As the moon, anguish'd, circles the earth:
Hopeless! abhorr'd! a death-shadow
Unseen, unbodied, unknown,
The mother of Pestilence.

9. But the fiery beam of Fuzon
Was a pillar of fire to Egypt
Five hundred years wand'ring on earth
Till Los siez'd it and beat in a mass
With the body of the sun.

Chap: II^d

1. But the forehead of Urizen gathering,
And his eyes pale with anguish, his lips
Blue & changing, in tears and bitter
Contrition, he prepar'd his Bow

2. Form'd of Ribs that in his dark solitude,
When obscur'd in his forests, fell monsters
Arose. For his dire Contemplations
Rush'd down like floods from his mountains,
In torrents of mud settling thick
With Eggs of unnatural production:
Forthwith hatching, some howl'd on his hills,
Some in vales, some aloft flew in air.

3. Of these, an enormous dread Serpent,
Scaled and poisonous horned,
Approach'd Urizen even to his knees
As he sat on his dark rooted Oak.

4. With his horns he push'd furious:
Great the conflict & great the jealousy
In cold poisons: but Urizen smote him.

5. First he poison'd the rocks with his blood,
Then polish'd his ribs, and his sinews
Dried, laid them apart till winter;
Then a Bow black prepar'd; on this Bow
A poisoned rock plac'd in silence.
He utter'd these words to the Bow:

6. 'O Bow of the clouds of secrecy,
O nerve of that lust form'd monster!
Send this rock swift invisible thro'
The black clouds on the bosom of Fuzon.'

7. So saying, In torment of his wounds,
He bent the enormous ribs slowly:
A circle of darkness! then fixed
The sinew in its rest; then the Rock,
Poisonous source! plac'd with art, lifting difficult
Its weighty bulk: silent the rock lay,

8. While Fuzon, his tygers unloosing,
Thought Urizen slain by his wrath.
'I am God,' said he, 'eldest of things!'

9. Sudden sings the rock: swift & invisible
On Fuzon flew: enter'd his bosom.
His beautiful visage, his tresses
That gave light to the mornings of heaven,
Were smitten with darkness, deform'd
And outstretch'd on the edge of the forest.

10. But the rock fell upon the Earth,
Mount Sinai in Arabia.

Chap: III

1. The Globe shook, and Urizen, seated
On black clouds, his sore wound anointed;
The ointment flow'd down on the void
Mix'd with blood: here the snake gets her poison.

2. With difficulty & great pain Urizen
Lifted on high the dead corse:
On his shoulders he bore it to where
A Tree hung over the Immensity.

3. For when Urizen shrunk away
From Eternals, he sat on a rock
Barren: a rock which himself
From redounding fancies had petrified.
Many tears fell on the rock,
Many sparks of vegetation.
Soon shot the pained root
Of Mystery under his heel.
It grew a thick tree: he wrote
In silence his book of iron,
Till the horrid plant, bending its boughs,
Grew to roots when it felt the earth
And again sprung to many a tree.

4. Amaz'd started Urizen! when
He beheld himself compassed round
And high roofed over with trees.
He arose, but the stems stood so thick
He with difficulty and great pain
Brought his Books, all but the Book
Of iron, from the dismal shade.

5. The Tree still grows over the Void,
Enrooting itself all around,
An endless labyrinth of woe!

6. The corse of his first begotten
On the accursed Tree of Mystery,
On the topmost stem of this Tree
Urizen nail'd Fuzon's corse.

Chap: IV

1. Forth flew the arrows of pestilence
Round the pale living Corse on the tree;

2. For in Urizen's slumbers of abstraction
In the infinite ages of Eternity,
When his Nerves of Joy melted and flow'd
A white Lake on the dark blue air,
In perturb'd pain and dismal torment
Now stretching out, now swift conglobing,

3. Effluvia vapour'd above
In noxious clouds; these hover'd thick
Over the disorganiz'd Immortal,
Till petrific pain scurf'd o'er the Lakes
As the bones of man, solid & dark.

4. The clouds of disease hover'd wide
Around the Immortal in torment,
Perching around the hurtling bones,
Disease on disease, shape on shape,
Winged, screaming in blood & torment.

5. The Eternal Prophet beat on his anvils,
Enrag'd in the desolate darkness,
He forg'd nets of iron around
And Los threw them around the bones.

6. The shapes screaming flutter'd vain:
Some combin'd into muscles & glands,
Some organs for craving and lust;
Most remain'd on the tormented void,
Urizen's army of horrors.

7. Round the pale living Corse on the Tree
Forty years flew the arrows of pestilence.

8. Wailing and terror and woe
Ran thro' all his dismal world
Forty years; all his sons & daughters
Felt their skulls harden; then Asia
Arose in the pendulous deep.

9. They reptilize upon the Earth.

10. Fuzon groan'd on the Tree.

Chap: V

1. The lamenting voice of Ahania
Weeping upon the void
And round the Tree of Fuzon:
Distant in solitary night
Her voice was heard, but no form
Had she; but her tears from clouds
Eternal fell round the Tree.

2. And the voice cried: 'Ah, Urizen! Love!
Flower of morning! I weep on the verge
Of Non-entity: how wide the Abyss
Between Ahania and thee!

3. 'I lie on the verge of the deep,
I see thy dark clouds ascend,
I see thy black forests and floods
A horrible waste to my eyes!

4. 'Weeping I walk over rocks,
Over dens & thro' valleys of death.
Why didst thou despise Ahania,
To cast me from thy bright presence
Into the World of Loneness?

5. 'I cannot touch his hand,
Nor weep on his knees, nor hear
His voice & bow, nor see his eyes
And joy, nor hear his footsteps and
My heart leap at the lovely sound!
I cannot kiss the place
Whereon his bright feet have trod,
But I wander on the rocks
With hard necessity.

6. 'Where is my golden palace?
Where my ivory bed?
Where the joy of my morning hour?
Where the sons of eternity singing

7. 'To awake bright Urizen, my king,
To arise to the mountain sport,
To the bliss of eternal valleys:

8. 'To awake my king in the morn
To embrace Ahania's joy
On the bredth of his open bosom,
From my soft cloud of dew to fall
In showers of life on his harvests?

9. 'When he gave my happy soul
To the sons of eternal joy:
When he took the daughters of life
Into my chambers of love:

10. 'When I found babes of bliss on my beds,
And bosoms of milk in my chambers
Fill'd with eternal seed,
O! eternal births sung round Ahania
In interchange sweet of their joys.

11. 'Swell'd with ripeness & fat with fatness,
Bursting on winds my odors,
My ripe figs and rich pomegranates
In infant joy at thy feet
O Urizen, sported and sang.

12. 'Then thou with thy lap full of seed,
With thy hand full of generous fire,
Walked forth from the clouds of morning,
On the virgins of springing joy,
On the human soul to cast
The seed of eternal science.

13. 'The sweat poured down thy temples
To Ahania return'd in evening;
The moisture awoke to birth
My mother's-joys, sleeping in bliss.

14. 'But now, alone, over rocks, mountains,
Cast out from thy lovely bosom,
Cruel jealousy, selfish fear,
Self-destroying: how can delight
Renew in these chains of darkness
Where bones of beasts are strown
On the bleak and snowy mountains
Where bones from the birth are buried
Before they see the light?'

FINIS

FROM *VALA,* OR *THE FOUR ZOAS*

from NIGHT THE NINTH

Luvah & Vala descended & enter'd the Gates of Dark Urthona,
And walk'd from the hands of Urizen in the shadows of Vala's Garden
Where the impressions of Despair & Hope for ever vegetate
In flowers, in fruits, in fishes, birds & beasts & clouds & waters,
The land of doubts & shadows, sweet delusions, unform'd hopes.
They saw no more the terrible confusion of the wracking universe.
They heard not, saw not, felt not all the terrible confusion,
For in their orbed senses, within clos'd up, they wander'd at will.
And those upon the Couches view'd them, in the dreams of Beulah,
As they repos'd from the terrible wide universal harvest,
Invisible Luvah in bright clouds hover'd over Vala's head,
And thus their ancient golden age renew'd; for Luvah spoke
With voice mild from his golden Cloud upon the breath of morning:

'Come forth, O Vala, from the grass & from the silent dew,
Rise from the dews of death, for the Eternal Man is Risen.'

She rises among flowers & looks toward the Eastern clearness
She walks yea runs, her feet are wing'd, on the tops of the bending
    grass,
Her garments rejoice in the vocal wind & her hair glistens with dew.

She answer'd thus: 'Whose voice is this, in the voice of the
    nourishing air,
In the spirit of the morning, awaking the Soul from its grassy bed?
Where dost thou dwell? for it is thee I seek, & but for thee
I must have slept Eternally, nor have felt the dew of thy morning.
Look how the opening dawn advances with vocal harmony!
Look how the beams foreshew the rising of some glorious power!
The sun is thine, he goeth forth in his majestic brightness.
O thou creating voice that callest! & who shall answer thee?'

'Where dost thou flee, O fair one? where doest thou seek thy
    happy place?'

'To yonder brightness, there I haste, for sure I came from thence
Or I must have slept eternally, nor have felt the dew of morning.'

'Eternally thou must have slept, nor have felt the morning dew,
But for yon nourishing sun; 'tis that by which thou art arisen.
The birds adore the sun: the beasts rise up & play in his beams,
And every flower & every leaf rejoices in his light.
Then, O thou fair one, sit thee down, for thou art as the grass,
Thou risest in the dew of morning & at night art folded up.'

   'Alas! am I but as a flower? then will I sit me down,
Then will I weep, then I'll complain & sigh for immortality,
And chide my maker, thee O Sun, that raisedst me to fall.'

So saying she sat down & wept beneath the apple trees.

'O be thou blotted out, thou Sun! that raisedst me to trouble,
That gavest me a heart to crave, & raisedst me, thy phantom,
To feel thy heat & see thy light & wander here alone,
Hopeless, if I am like the grass & so shall pass away.'

'Rise, sluggish Soul, why sit'st thou here? why dost thou sit & weep
Yon sun shall wax old & decay, but thou shalt ever flourish.
The fruit shall ripen & fall down, & the flowers consume away,
But thou shalt still survive; arise, O dry thy dewy tears.'

'Hah! shall I still survive? whence came that sweet & comforting
    voice?
And whence that voice of sorrow? O sun! thou art nothing now
    to me.
Go on thy course rejoicing, & let us both rejoice together.
I walk among his flocks & hear the bleating of his lambs
O that I could behold his face & follow his pure feet!

I walk by the footsteps of his flocks; come hither, tender flocks.
Can you converse with a pure soul that seeketh for her maker?
You answer not: then am I set your mistress in this garden.
I'll watch you & attend your footsteps; you are not like the birds.
That sing & fly in the bright air; but you do lick my feet
And let me touch your woolly backs; follow me as I sing,
For in my bosom a new song arises to my Lord:

'Rise up, O sun, most glorious minister & light of day.
Flow on, ye gentle airs, & bear the voice of my rejoicing.
Wave freshly, clear waters flowing around the tender grass;
And thou, sweet smelling ground, put forth thy life in fruits &
    flowers.
Follow me, O my flocks, & hear me sing my rapturous song.
I will cause my voice to be heard on the clouds that glitter in the
    sun.
I will call; & who shall answer me? I will sing; who shall reply?
For from my pleasant hills behold the living, living springs,
Running among my green pastures, delighting among my trees,
I am not here alone: my flocks, you are my brethren;
And you birds that sing & adorn the sky, you are my sisters.
I sing, & you reply to my song; I rejoice, & you are glad.
Follow me, O my flocks; we will now descend into the valley.
O how delicious are the grapes, flourishing in the sun!
How clear the spring of the rock, running among the golden sand!
How cool the breezes of the valley, & the arms of the branching
    trees!
Cover us from the sun; come & let us sit in the shade.
My Luvah here hath plac'd me in a sweet & pleasant land,
And given me fruits & pleasant waters, & warm hills & cool valleys.
Here will I build myself a house, & here I'll call on his name,
Here I'll return when I am weary & take my pleasant rest.'

So spoke the sinless soul, & laid her head on the downy fleece
Of a curl'd Ram who stretch'd himself in sleep beside his mistress,
And soft sleep fell upon her eyelids in the silent noon of day.

The Sun has left his blackness & has found a fresher morning,
And the mild moon rejoices in the clear & cloudless night,
And Man walks forth from midst of the fires: the evil is all
    consum'd.
His eyes behold the Angelic spheres arising night & day;
The stars consum'd like a lamp blown out, & in their stead,
    behold
The Expanding Eyes of Man behold the depths of wondrous
    worlds!
One Earth, one sea beneath; nor Erring Globes wander, but Stars
Of fire rise up nightly from the Ocean; & one Sun
Each morning, like a New born Man, issues with songs & joy
Calling the Plowman to his Labour & the Shepherd to his rest.
He walks upon the Eternal Mountains, raising his heavenly voice,
Conversing with the Animal forms of wisdom night & day,
That, risen from the Sea of fire, renew'd walk o'er the Earth;
For Tharmas brought his flocks upon the hills, & in the Vales
Around the Eternal Man's bright tent, the little Children play
Among the wooly flocks. The hammer of Urthona sounds
In the deep caves beneath; his limbs renew'd, his Lions roar
Around the Furnaces & in Evening sport upon the plains.
They raise their faces from the Earth, conversing with the Man:

'How is it we have walk'd thro' fires & yet are not consum'd?
How is it that all things are chang'd, even as in ancient times?'

The Sun arises from his dewy bed, & the fresh airs
Play in his smiling beams giving the seeds of life to grow,
And the fresh Earth beams forth ten thousand thousand springs of
    life.
Urthona is arisen in his strength, no longer now
Divided from Enitharmon, no longer the Spectre Los.
Where is the Spectre of Prophecy? where the delusive Phantom?
Departed: & Urthona rises from the ruinous Walls

In all his ancient strength to form the golden armour of science
For intellectual War. The war of swords departed now,
The dark Religions are departed & sweet Science reigns.

End of The Dream

ALL RELIGIONS ARE ONE

The Voice of one crying in the Wilderness.

The Argument

As the true method of knowledge is experiment, the true faculty of knowing must be the faculty which experiences. This faculty I treat of.

Principle 1st

That the Poetic Genius is the true Man, and that the body or outward form of Man is derived from the Poetic Genius. Likewise that the forms of all things are derived from their Genius, which by the Ancients was call'd an Angel & Spirit & Demon.

Principle 2d

As all men are alike in outward form, So (and with the same infinite variety) all are alike in the Poetic Genius.

Principle 3d

No man can think, write, or speak from his heart, but he must intend truth. Thus all sects of Philosophy are from the Poetic Genius adapted to the weaknesses of every individual.

Principle 4th

As none by traveling over known lands can find out the unknown, So, from already acquired knowledge, Man could not acquire more; therefore an universal Poetic Genius exists.

Principle 5th

The Religions of all Nations are derived from each Nation's different reception of the Poetic Genius, which is every where call'd the Spirit of Prophecy.

Principle 6th

The Jewish & Christian Testaments are An original derivation from the Poetic Genius: this is necessary from the confined nature of bodily sensation.

Principle 7th

As all men are alike (tho' infinitely various), So all Religions, &, as all similars, have one source.

The true Man is the source, he being the Poetic Genius.

THERE IS NO NATURAL RELIGION

[a]
The Argument

Man has no notion of moral fitness but from Education. Naturally he is only a natural organ subject to Sense.

I

Man cannot naturally Percieve but through his natural or bodily organs.

II

Man by his reasoning power can only compare & judge of what he has already perciev'd.

III

From a perception of only 3 senses or 3 elements none could deduce a fourth or fifth.

IV

None could have other than natural or organic thoughts if he had none but organic perceptions.

V

Man's desires are limited by his perceptions: none can desire what he has not perciev'd.

VI

The desires & perceptions of man untaught by any thing but organs of sense, must be limited to objects of sense.

Conclusion

If it were not for the Poetic or Prophetic Character, the Philosophic & Experimental would soon be at the ratio of all things & stand still, unable to do other than repeat the same dull round over again.

[*b*]

I

Man's perceptions are not bounded by organs of perception: he percieves more than sense (tho' ever so acute) can discover.

II

Reason, or the ratio of all we have already known, is not the same that it shall be when we know more.

III

[*This proposition is missing.*]

IV

The bounded is loathed by its possessor. The same dull round, even of a universe, would soon become a mill with complicated wheels.

V

If the many become the same as the few when possess'd, More! More! is the cry of a mistaken soul: less than All cannot satisfy Man.

VI

If any could desire what he is incapable of possessing, despair must be his eternal lot.

VII

The desire of Man being Infinite, the possession is Infinite & himself Infinite.

Application

He who sees the Infinite in all things, sees God. He who sees the Ratio only, sees himself only.

Therefore God becomes as we are, that we may be as he is.

SONGS OF INNOCENCE

Introduction

Piping down the valleys wild,
Piping songs of pleasant glee,
On a cloud I saw a child,
And he laughing said to me:

'Pipe a song about a Lamb!'
So I piped with merry chear.
'Piper, pipe that song again;'
So I piped: he wept to hear.

'Drop thy pipe, thy happy pipe,
Sing thy songs of happy chear.'
So I sung the same again
While he wept with joy to hear.

'Piper, sit thee down and write
In a book that all may read.'
So he vanish'd from my sight,
And I pluck'd a hollow reed,

And I made a rural pen,
And I stain'd the water clear,
And I wrote my happy songs
Every child may joy to hear.

The Shepherd

How sweet is the Shepherd's sweet lot!
From the morn to the evening he strays;
He shall follow his sheep all the day,
And his tongue shall be filled with praise.

For he hears the lamb's innocent call,
And he hears the ewe's tender reply;
He is watchful, while they are in peace,
For they know when their Shepherd is nigh.

The Ecchoing Green

The Sun does arise
And make happy the skies,
The merry bells ring
To welcome the Spring,
The sky-lark and thrush,
The birds of the bush,
Sing louder around
To the bells' chearful sound,
While our sports shall be seen
On the Ecchoing Green.

Old John with white hair
Does laugh away care,
Sitting under the oak
Among the old folk.
They laugh at our play,
And soon they all say:
'Such, such were the joys
When we all, girls & boys,
In our youth-time were seen
On the Ecchoing Green.'

Till the little ones, weary,
No more can be merry;
The sun does descend,
And our sports have an end.
Round the laps of their mothers
Many sisters and brothers,
Like birds in their nest,
Are ready for rest,
And sport no more seen
On the darkening Green.

The Lamb

Little Lamb, who made thee:
Dost thou know who made thee?
Gave thee life & bid thee feed
By the stream & o'er the mead;
Gave thee clothing of delight,
Softest clothing, wooly, bright;
Gave thee such a tender voice
Making all the vales rejoice?
Little Lamb, who made thee?
Dost thou know who made thee?

Little Lamb, I'll tell thee,
Little Lamb, I'll tell thee:
He is called by thy name,
For he calls himself a Lamb.
He is meek & he is mild;
He became a little child:
I a child & thou a lamb,
We are called by his name.
Little Lamb, God bless thee.
Little Lamb, God bless thee.

The Little Black Boy

My mother bore me in the southern wild,
And I am black, but O! my soul is white;
White as an angel is the English child,
But I am black, as if bereav'd of light.

My mother taught me underneath a tree,
And sitting down before the heat of day
She took me on her lap and kissed me,
And pointing to the east, began to say:

'Look on the rising sun! there God does live,
And gives his light and gives his heat away;
And flowers and trees and beasts and men recieve
Comfort in morning, joy in the noon day.

'And we are put on earth a little space
That we may learn to bear the beams of love;
And these black bodies and this sun-burnt face
Is but a cloud, and like a shady grove;

'For when our souls have learn'd the heat to bear,
The cloud will vanish: we shall hear his voice,
Saying: "come out from the grove, my love & care,
And round my golden tent like lambs rejoice."'

Thus did my mother say, and kissed me.
And thus I say to little English boy:
When I from black and he from white cloud free
And round the tent of God like lambs we joy,

I'll shade him from the heat, till he can bear
To lean in joy upon our father's knee;
And then I'll stand and stroke his silver hair,
And be like him, and he will then love me.

The Blossom

Merry Merry Sparrow,
Under leaves so green,
A happy Blossom
Sees you swift as arrow
Seek your cradle narrow
Near my Bosom.

Pretty Pretty Robin,
Under leaves so green,
A happy Blossom
Hears you sobbing, sobbing.
Pretty Pretty Robin
Near my Bosom.

The Chimney Sweeper

When my mother died I was very young,
And my father sold me while yet my tongue
Could scarcely cry 'weep, weep, weep, weep,'
So your chimneys I sweep & in soot I sleep.

There's little Tom Dacre who cried when his head,
That curl'd like a lamb's back, was shav'd: so I said,
'Hush, Tom, never mind it, for when your head's bare
You know that the soot cannot spoil your white hair.'

And so he was quiet, & that very night,
As Tom was a sleeping, he had such a sight,
That thousands of sweepers, Dick, Joe, Ned & Jack,
Were all of them lock'd up in coffins of black.

And by came an Angel who had a bright key,
And he open'd the coffins & set them all free;
Then down a green plain, leaping, laughing, they run,
And wash in a river, and shine in the Sun.

Then naked & white, all their bags left behind,
They rise upon clouds, and sport in the wind;
And the Angel told Tom, if he'd be a good boy,
He'd have God for his father & never want joy.

And so Tom awoke; and we rose in the dark,
And got with our bags & our brushes to work.
Tho' the morning was cold, Tom was happy & warm;
So if all do their duty they need not fear harm.

The Little Boy Lost

'Father, father, where are you going?
O do not walk so fast.
Speak father, speak to your little boy,
Or else I shall be lost.'

The night was dark, no father was there;
The child was wet with dew;
The mire was deep, & the child did weep,
And away the vapour flew.

The Little Boy Found

The little boy lost in the lonely fen,
Led by the wand'ring light,
Began to cry, but God ever nigh,
Appear'd like his father in white.

He kissed the child & by the hand led
And to his mother brought,
Who in sorrow pale, thro' the lonely dale,
Her little boy weeping sought.

Laughing Song

When the green woods laugh with the voice of joy,
And the dimpling stream runs laughing by,
When the air does laugh with our merry wit,
And the green hill laughs with the noise of it,

When the meadows laugh with lively green,
And the grasshopper laughs in the merry scene,
When Mary and Susan and Emily
With their sweet round mouths sing 'Ha, Ha, He!'

When the painted birds laugh in the shade
Where our table with cherries and nuts is spread,
Come live & be merry and join with me,
To sing the sweet chorus of 'Ha, Ha, He!'

A CRADLE SONG

Sweet dreams, form a shade
O'er my lovely infant's head,
Sweet dreams of pleasant streams
By happy silent moony beams.

Sweet sleep, with soft down
Weave thy brows an infant crown.
Sweet sleep, Angel mild,
Hover o'er my happy child.

Sweet smiles, in the night
Hover over my delight;
Sweet smiles, Mother's smiles,
All the livelong night beguiles.

Sweet moans, dovelike sighs
Chase not slumber from thy eyes.
Sweet moans, sweeter smiles
All the dovelike moans beguiles.

Sleep, sleep, happy child,
All creation slept and smil'd;
Sleep, sleep, happy sleep,
While o'er thee thy mother weep.

Sweet babe, in thy face
Holy image I can trace.
Sweet babe, once like thee
Thy maker lay and wept for me:

Wept for me, for thee, for all,
When he was an infant small.
Thou his image ever see,
Heavenly face that smiles on thee:

Smiles on thee, on me, on all,
Who became an infant small.
Infant smiles are his own smiles,
Heaven & earth to peace beguiles.

The Divine Image

To Mercy Pity Peace and Love
All pray in their distress,
And to these virtues of delight
Return their thankfulness.

For Mercy Pity Peace and Love
Is God our father dear,
And Mercy Pity Peace and Love
Is Man his child and care.

For Mercy has a human heart,
Pity, a human face,
And Love, the human form divine,
And Peace, the human dress.

Then every man of every clime
That prays in his distress,
Prays to the human form divine,
Love Mercy Pity Peace.

And all must love the human form
In heathen, turk or jew.
Where Mercy Love & Pity dwell
There God is dwelling too.

HOLY THURSDAY

'Twas on a Holy Thursday, their innocent faces clean,
The children walking two & two, in red & blue & green,
Grey headed beadles walk'd before, with wands as white as snow,
Till into the high dome of Paul's they like Thames' waters flow.

O what a multitude they seem'd, these flowers of London town!
Seated in companies they sit with radiance all their own.
The hum of multitudes was there, but multitudes of lambs,
Thousands of little boys & girls raising their innocent hands.

Now like a mighty wind they raise to heaven the voice of song,
Or like harmonious thunderings the seats of heaven among.
Beneath them sit the aged men, wise guardians of the poor;
Then cherish pity, lest you drive an angel from your door.

Night

The sun descending in the west
The evening star does shine,
The birds are silent in their nest
And I must seek for mine,
The moon, like a flower
In heaven's high bower,
With silent delight
Sits and smiles on the night.

Farewell green fields and happy groves
Where flocks have took delight;
Where lambs have nibbled, silent moves
The feet of angels bright;
Unseen they pour blessing
And joy without ceasing
On each bud and blossom
And each sleeping bosom.

They look in every thoughtless nest
Where birds are cover'd warm,
They visit caves of every beast
To keep them all from harm;
If they see any weeping
That should have been sleeping,
They pour sleep on their head
And sit down by their bed.

When wolves and tygers howl for prey
They pitying stand and weep,
Seeking to drive their thirst away
And keep them from the sheep;
But if they rush dreadful,
The angels most heedful
Recieve each mild spirit
New worlds to inherit.

And there the lion's ruddy eyes
Shall flow with tears of gold,
And pitying the tender cries
And walking round the fold
Saying, 'wrath, by his meekness,
And by his health, sickness
Is driven away
From our immortal day.

'And now beside thee, bleating lamb,
I can lie down and sleep,
Or think on him who bore thy name,
Graze after thee and weep;
For, wash'd in life's river,
My bright mane for ever
Shall shine like the gold
As I guard o'er the fold.'

Spring

Sound the Flute!
Now it's mute.
Birds delight
Day and Night;
Nightingale
In the dale,
Lark in Sky,
Merrily,
Merrily, Merrily, to welcome in the Year.

Little Boy
Full of joy,
Little Girl
Sweet and small,
Cock does crow,
So do you;
Merry voice,
Infant noise,
Merrily, Merrily, to welcome in the Year.

Little Lamb
Here I am,
Come and lick
My white neck,
Let me pull
Your soft Wool,
Let me kiss
Your soft face;
Merrily, Merrily, we welcome in the Year.

Nurse's Song

When the voices of children are heard on the green
And laughing is heard on the hill,
My heart is at rest within my breast
And every thing else is still.

'Then come home, my children, the sun is gone down
And the dews of night arise;
Come, come, leave off play, and let us away
Till the morning appears in the skies.'

'No, no, let us play, for it is yet day
And we cannot go to sleep;
Besides, in the sky the little birds fly
And the hills are all cover'd with sheep.'

'Well, well, go & play till the light fades away
And then go home to bed.'
The little ones leaped & shouted & laugh'd
And all the hills ecchoed.

Infant Joy

'I have no name:
I am but two days old.'
What shall I call thee?
'I happy am,
Joy is my name.'
Sweet joy befall thee!

Pretty joy!
Sweet joy but two days old,
Sweet joy I call thee:
Thou dost smile,
I sing the while
Sweet joy befall thee.

A Dream

Once a dream did weave a shade
O'er my Angel-guarded bed,
That an Emmet lost its way
Where on grass methought I lay.

Troubled, 'wilder'd and folorn,
Dark, benighted, travel-worn,
Over many a tangled spray,
All heart-broke I heard her say:

'O my children! do they cry?
Do they hear their father sigh?
Now they look abroad to see,
Now return and weep for me.'

Pitying, I dropp'd a tear;
But I saw a glow-worm near,
Who replied: 'What wailing wight
Calls the watchman of the night?

'I am set to light the ground,
While the beetle goes his round:
Follow now the beetle's hum;
Little wanderer, hie thee home.'

On Another's Sorrow

Can I see another's woe
And not be in sorrow too?
Can I see another's grief
And not seek for kind relief?

Can I see a falling tear
And not feel my sorrow's share?
Can a father see his child
Weep, nor be with sorrow fill'd?

Can a mother sit and hear
An infant groan an infant fear?
No, no never can it be,
Never, never can it be.

And can he who smiles on all
Hear the wren with sorrows small,
Hear the small bird's grief & care,
Hear the woes that infants bear,

And not sit beside the nest
Pouring pity in their breast,
And not sit the cradle near
Weeping tear on infant's tear,

And not sit both night & day
Wiping all our tears away?
O! no never can it be,
Never, never can it be.

He doth give his joy to all,
He becomes an infant small,
He becomes a man of woe,
He doth feel the sorrow too.

Think not thou canst sigh a sigh
And thy maker is not by;
Think not thou canst weep a tear
And thy maker is not near.

O! he gives to us his joy
That our grief he may destroy;
Till our grief is fled & gone
He doth sit by us and moan.

SONGS OF EXPERIENCE

Introduction

Hear the voice of the Bard!
Who Present, Past, & Future sees,
Whose ears have heard
The Holy Word
That walk'd among the ancient trees,

Calling the lapsed Soul,
And weeping in the evening dew,
That might controll
The starry pole
And fallen fallen light renew!

'O Earth, O Earth return!
Arise from out the dewy grass;
Night is worn
And the morn
Rises from the slumberous mass.

'Turn away no more:
Why wilt thou turn away?
The starry floor
The wat'ry shore
Is giv'n thee till the break of day.'

EARTH'S Answer

Earth rais'd up her head
From the darkness dread & drear.
Her light fled:
Stony dread!
And her locks cover'd with grey despair.

'Prison'd on wat'ry shore,
Starry Jealousy does keep my den
Cold and hoar;
Weeping o'er,
I hear the father of the ancient men.

'Selfish father of men,
Cruel, jealous, selfish fear:
Can delight,
Chain'd in night,
The virgins of youth and morning bear?

'Does spring hide its joy
When buds and blossoms grow?
Does the sower
Sow by night?
Or the plowman in darkness plow?

'Break this heavy chain
That does freeze my bones around.
Selfish! vain!
Eternal bane!
That free Love with bondage bound.'

The CLOD & the PEBBLE

'Love seeketh not Itself to please
Nor for itself hath any care,
But for another gives its ease
And builds a Heaven in Hell's despair.'

So sung a little Clod of Clay
Trodden with the cattle's feet,
But a Pebble of the brook
Warbled out these metres meet:

'Love seeketh only Self to please,
To bind another to Its delight,
Joys in another's loss of ease,
And builds a Hell in Heaven's despite.'

HOLY THURSDAY

Is this a holy thing to see
In a rich and fruitful land,
Babes reduc'd to misery,
Fed with cold and usurous hand?

Is that trembling cry a song?
Can it be a song of joy?
And so many children poor?
It is a land of poverty!

And their sun does never shine,
And their fields are bleak & bare,
And their ways are fill'd with thorns:
It is eternal winter there.

For where-e'er the sun does shine,
And where-e'er the rain does fall,
Babe can never hunger there,
Nor poverty the mind appall.

The Little Girl Lost

In futurity
I prophetic see
That the earth from sleep
(Grave the sentence deep)

Shall arise and seek
For her maker meek,
And the desart wild
Become a garden mild.

In the southern clime
Where the summer's prime
Never fades away,
Lovely Lyca lay.

Seven summers old
Lovely Lyca told;
She had wander'd long
Hearing wild birds' song.

'Sweet sleep, come to me
Underneath this tree.
Do father, mother, weep,
Where can Lyca sleep?

'Lost in desart wild
Is your little child.
How can Lyca sleep
If her mother weep?

'If her heart does ake
Then let Lyca wake;
If my mother sleep,
Lyca shall not weep.

'Frowning frowning night,
O'er this desart bright
Let thy moon arise
While I close my eyes.'

Sleeping Lyca lay
While the beasts of prey,
Come from caverns deep,
View'd the maid asleep.

The kingly lion stood
And the virgin view'd,
Then he gambol'd round
O'er the hallow'd ground.

Leopards, tygers play
Round her as she lay,
While the lion old
Bow'd his mane of gold,

And her bosom lick,
And upon her neck
From his eyes of flame
Ruby tears there came;

While the lioness
Loos'd her slender dress,
And naked they convey'd
To caves the sleeping maid.

The Little Girl Found

All the night in woe
Lyca's parents go
Over vallies deep,
While the desarts weep.

Tired and woe-begone,
Hoarse with making moan,
Arm in arm seven days
They trac'd the desart ways.

Seven nights they sleep
Among shadows deep,
And dream they see their child
Starv'd in desert wild.

Pale, thro' pathless ways
The fancied image strays,
Famish'd, weeping, weak
With hollow piteous shriek.

Rising from unrest,
The trembling woman prest
With feet of weary woe:
She could no further go.

In his arms he bore
Her arm'd with sorrow sore,
Till before their way
A couching lion lay.

Turning back was vain:
Soon his heavy mane
Bore them to the ground,
Then he stalk'd around

Smelling to his prey,
But their fears allay
When he licks their hands
And silent by them stands.

They look upon his eyes
Fill'd with deep surprise,
And wondering behold
A spirit arm'd in gold.

On his head a crown,
On his shoulders down
Flow'd his golden hair.
Gone was all their care.

'Follow me,' he said;
'Weep not for the maid;
In my palace deep
Lyca lies asleep.'

Then they followed
Where the vision led,
And saw their sleeping child
Among tygers wild.

To this day they dwell
In a lonely dell,
Nor fear the wolvish howl
Nor the lion's growl.

The Chimney Sweeper

A little black thing among the snow,
Crying 'weep, weep,' in notes of woe!
'Where are thy father & mother, say?'
'They are both gone up to the church to pray.

'Because I was happy upon the heath,
And smil'd among the winter's snow,
They clothed me in the clothes of death,
And taught me to sing the notes of woe.

'And because I am happy, & dance & sing,
They think they have done me no injury,
And are gone to praise God & his Priest & King,
Who make up a heaven of our misery.'

NURSE'S Song

When the voices of children are heard on the green
And whisp'rings are in the dale,
The days of my youth rise fresh in my mind:
My face turns green and pale.

Then come home my children, the sun is gone down
And the dews of night arise;
Your spring & your day are wasted in play,
And your winter and night in disguise.

The SICK ROSE

O Rose, thou art sick:
The invisible worm
That flies in the night
In the howling storm,

Has found out thy bed
Of crimson joy,
And his dark secret love
Does thy life destroy.

THE FLY

Little Fly,
Thy summer's play
My thoughtless hand
Has brush'd away.

Am not I
A fly like thee?
Or art not thou
A man like me?

For I dance
And drink & sing,
Till some blind hand
Shall brush my wing.

If thought is life
And strength & breath,
And the want
Of thought is death,

Then am I
A happy fly
If I live
Or if I die.

The Angel

I dreamt a Dream! what can it mean?
And that I was a maiden Queen
Guarded by an Angel mild:
Witless woe was ne'er beguil'd!

And I wept both night and day,
And he wip'd my tears away,
And I wept both day and night,
And hid from him my heart's delight.

So he took his wings and fled;
Then the morn blush'd rosy red;
I dried my tears & arm'd my fears
With ten thousand shields and spears.

Soon my Angel came again:
I was arm'd, he came in vain,
For the time of youth was fled
And grey hairs were on my head.

The Tyger

Tyger, Tyger, burning bright
In the forests of the night,
What immortal hand or eye
Could frame thy fearful symmetry?

In what distant deeps or skies
Burnt the fire of thine eyes?
On what wings dare he aspire?
What the hand dare sieze the fire?

And what shoulder, & what art,
Could twist the sinews of thy heart?
And when thy heart began to beat,
What dread hand? & what dread feet?

What the hammer? what the chain,
In what furnace was thy brain?
What the anvil? what dread grasp
Dare its deadly terrors clasp?

When the stars threw down their spears
And water'd heaven with their tears,
Did he smile his work to see?
Did he who made the Lamb make thee?

Tyger, Tyger, burning bright
In the forests of the night,
What immortal hand or eye
Dare frame thy fearful symmetry?

My Pretty ROSE TREE

A flower was offer'd to me,
Such a flower as May never bore;
But I said 'I've a Pretty Rose-tree,'
And I passed the sweet flower o'er.

Then I went to my Pretty Rose-tree,
To tend her by day and by night;
But my Rose turn'd away with jealousy,
And her thorns were my only delight.

AH! SUN-FLOWER

Ah Sun-flower! weary of time,
Who countest the steps of the Sun,
Seeking after that sweet golden clime
Where the traveller's journey is done:

Where the Youth pined away with desire,
And the pale Virgin shrouded in snow,
Arise from their graves and aspire
Where my Sun-flower wishes to go.

THE LILLY

The modest Rose puts forth a thorn,
The humble Sheep a threat'ning horn,
While the Lilly white shall in Love delight,
Nor a thorn nor a threat stain her beauty bright.

The GARDEN of LOVE

I went to the Garden of Love,
And saw what I never had seen:
A Chapel was built in the midst,
Where I used to play on the green.

And the gates of this Chapel were shut,
And 'Thou shalt not' writ over the door;
So I turn'd to the Garden of Love
That so many sweet flowers bore;

And I saw it was filled with graves,
And tomb-stones where flowers should be;
And Priests in black gowns were walking their rounds,
And binding with briars my joys & desires.

The Little Vagabond

Dear Mother, dear Mother, the Church is cold,
But the Ale-house is healthy & pleasant & warm;
Besides I can tell where I am used well,
Such usage in heaven will never do well.

But if at the Church they would give us some Ale
And a pleasant fire our souls to regale,
We'd sing and we'd pray all the live-long day,
Nor ever once wish from the Church to stray.

Then the Parson might preach & drink & sing,
And we'd be as happy as birds in the spring;
And modest dame Lurch, who is always at Church,
Would not have bandy children, nor fasting, nor birch.

And God, like a father rejoicing to see
His children as pleasant and happy as he,
Would have no more quarrel with the Devil or the Barrel,
But kiss him & give him both drink and apparel.

LONDON

I wander thro' each charter'd street
Near where the charter'd Thames does flow,
And mark in every face I meet
Marks of weakness, marks of woe.

In every cry of every Man,
In every Infant's cry of fear,
In every voice, in every ban,
The mind-forg'd manacles I hear.

How the Chimney-sweeper's cry
Every black'ning Church appalls,
And the hapless Soldier's sigh
Runs in blood down Palace walls.

But most thro' midnight streets I hear
How the youthful Harlot's curse
Blasts the new born Infant's tear,
And blights with plagues the Marriage hearse.

The Human Abstract

Pity would be no more
If we did not make somebody Poor;
And Mercy no more could be
If all were as happy as we.

And mutual fear brings peace,
Till the selfish loves increase:
Then Cruelty knits a snare
And spreads his baits with care.

He sits down with holy fears
And waters the ground with tears:
Then Humility takes its root
Underneath his foot.

Soon spreads the dismal shade
Of Mystery over his head,
And the Catterpiller and Fly
Feed on the Mystery.

And it bears the fruit of Deceit,
Ruddy and sweet to eat,
And the Raven his nest has made
In its thickest shade.

The Gods of the earth and sea
Sought thro' Nature to find this Tree,
But their search was all in vain:
There grows one in the Human Brain.

INFANT SORROW

My mother groan'd! my father wept,
Into the dangerous world I leapt,
Helpless, naked, piping loud,
Like a fiend hid in a cloud.

Struggling in my father's hands,
Striving against my swadling bands,
Bound and weary, I thought best
To sulk upon my mother's breast.

A POISON TREE

I was angry with my friend,
I told my wrath, my wrath did end;
I was angry with my foe,
I told it not, my wrath did grow.

And I water'd it in fears,
Night & morning with my tears;
And I sunned it with smiles,
And with soft deceitful wiles.

And it grew both day and night,
Till it bore an apple bright;
And my foe beheld it shine,
And he knew that it was mine,

And into my garden stole
When the night had veil'd the pole:
In the morning glad I see
My foe outstretch'd beneath the tree.

A Little BOY Lost

'Nought loves another as itself,
Nor venerates another so,
Nor is it possible to Thought
A greater than itself to know:

'And Father, how can I love you
Or any of my brothers more?
I love you like the little bird
That picks up crumbs around the door.'

The Priest sat by and heard the child,
In trembling zeal he siez'd his hair:
He led him by his little coat,
And all admir'd the Priestly care.

And standing on the altar high,
'Lo, what a fiend is here!' said he,
'One who sets reason up for judge
Of our most holy Mystery.'

The weeping child could not be heard,
The weeping parents wept in vain;
They strip'd him to his little shirt,
And bound him in an iron chain;

And burn'd him in a holy place,
Where many had been burn'd before:
The weeping parents wept in vain.
Are such things done on Albion's shore?

A Little GIRL Lost

Children of the future Age
Reading this indignant page,
Know that in a former time
Love! sweet Love! was thought a crime.

In the Age of Gold,
Free from winter's cold,
Youth and maiden bright
To the holy light,
Naked in the sunny beams delight.

Once a youthful pair,
Fill'd with softest care,
Met in garden bright
Where the holy light
Had just remov'd the curtains of the night.

There, in rising day,
On the grass they play;
Parents were afar,
Strangers came not near,
And the maiden soon forgot her fear.

Tired with kisses sweet,
They agree to meet
When the silent sleep
Waves o'er heaven's deep,
And the weary tired wanderers weep.

To her father white
Came the maiden bright;
But his loving look,
Like the holy book,
All her tender limbs with terror shook.

'Ona! pale and weak!
To thy father speak:
O the trembling fear!
O the dismal care!
That shakes the blossoms of my hoary hair.'

To Tirzah

Whater'er is Born of Mortal Birth
Must be consumed with the Earth
To rise from Generation free:
Then what have I to do with thee?

The Sexes sprung from Shame & Pride,
Blow'd in the morn, in evening died;
But Mercy chang'd Death into Sleep;
The Sexes rose to work & weep.

Thou Mother of my Mortal part,
With cruelty didst mould my Heart,
And with false self-decieving tears
Didst bind my Nostrils Eyes & Ears:

Didst close my Tongue in senseless clay,
And me to Mortal Life betray.
The Death of Jesus set me free:
Then what have I to do with thee?

The School Boy

I love to rise in a summer morn
When the birds sing on every tree;
The distant huntsman winds his horn,
And the sky-lark sings with me.
O! what sweet company.

But to go to school in a summer morn,
O! it drives all joy away;
Under a cruel eye outworn
The little ones spend the day
In sighing and dismay.

Ah! then at times I drooping sit,
And spend many an anxious hour,
Nor in my book can I take delight,
Nor sit in learning's bower,
Worn thro' with the dreary shower.

How can the bird that is born for joy
Sit in a cage and sing?
How can a child when fears annoy
But droop his tender wing
And forget his youthful spring?

O! father & mother, if buds are nip'd
And blossoms blown away,
And if the tender plants are strip'd
Of their joy in the springing day,
By sorrow and care's dismay,

How shall the summer arise in joy,
Or the summer fruits appear?
Or how shall we gather what griefs destroy,
Or bless the mellowing year
When the blasts of winter appear?

The Voice of the Ancient Bard

Youth of delight, come hither
And see the opening morn,
Image of truth new born.
Doubt is fled & clouds of reason,
Dark disputes & artful teazing.
Folly is an endless maze,
Tangled roots perplex her ways,
How many have fallen there!
They stumble all night over bones of the dead,
And feel they know not what but care,
And wish to lead others when they should be led.

A Divine Image*

Cruelty has a Human Heart,
And Jealousy a Human Face;
Terror the Human Form Divine,
And Secrecy the Human Dress.

The Human Dress is forged Iron,
The Human Form a fiery Forge,
The Human Face a Furnace seal'd,
The Human Heart its hungry Gorge.

*'A Divine Image' was etched by Blake in about 1791 but not included
by him in any copy of *Songs of Experience*.

For. the Sexes

The Gates of Paradise

Mutual Forgiveness of each Vice
Such are the Gates of Paradise
Against the Accusers chief desire
Who walkd among the Stones of Fire
Jehovahs Finger Wrote the Law
Then Wept: then rose in Zeal & Awe
And the Dead Corpse from Sinais heat
Buried beneath his Mercy Seat,
O Christians Christians: tell me Why
You rear it on your Altars high

What is Man

The Suns Light when he unfolds it
Depends on the Organ that beholds it
Publishd by WBlake 17 May 1793

I found him beneath a Tree ~

Publish'd 17 May 1793 by W Blake

2 **Water**
Thou Waterest him with Tears
Published by WBlake 17 May 1793

134

3   **Earth**
He struggles into Life
Publish'd by WBlake 17 May 1793

Air

4   On Cloudy Doubts & Reasoning Cares.
Publishd 17 May 1793 by WBlake Lambeth

Fire *That end in endless Strife*

Pub by W Blake 17 May 1793

5

At length for hatching ripe
he breaks the shell
6
Published by WBlake 17 May 1793

7 What are these? Alas! the Female Martyr
Is She also the Divine Image.

Publishd 17 May 1793 by WBlake Lambeth

8   My Son! my Son!

Publishd by WBlake 17 May 1793 Lambeth

9   I want! I want!

Pub.ᵈ by WBlake 17 May 1793

10 Help! Help!

Poblishd by W Blake 17 May 1793

Aged Ignorance

"Perceptive Organs closed their Objects close

Published 17 May 1793 by W Blake Lambeth.

12 Does thy God O Priest take such vengeance
as this?
Publishd 17 May 1793 by W Blake Lambeth

13   Fear & Hope are — Vision

The Traveller hasteth in the
Evening

14

Publishd 17 May 1793 by W Blake Lambeth

146

15   Death's Door

Publishd 1 May 1793 by WBlake Lambeth

16 I have said to the Worm: Thou
    art my mother & my sister
    Published by W Blake 1793 May 1793

The Keys

The Catterpiller on the Leaf
Reminds thee of thy Mothers Grief

of the Gates

1 My Eternal Man set in Repose
The Female from his darkness rose
And She found me beneath a Tree
A Mandrake & in her Veil hid me
Serpent Reasonings us entice
Of Good & Evil. Virtue & Vice
2 Doubt Self Jealous Watry folly
3 Struggling thro Earths Melancholy
4 Naked in Air in Shame & Fear
5 Blind in Fire with shield & spear
Two Hornd Reasoning Cloven Fiction
In Doubt which is Self contradiction
A dark Hermaphrodite We stood
Rational Truth Root of Evil & Good
Round me flew the Flaming Sword
Round her snowy Whirlwinds roard
Freezing her Veil the Mundane Shell
6 I rent the Veil where the Dead dwell
When weary Man enters his Cave

17

149

He meets his Saviour in the Grave.
Some find a Female Garment there
And some a Male, woven with care
Lest the Sexual Garments sweet
Should grow a devouring Winding sheet
7 One Dies! Alas! the Living & Dead
One is slain & One is fled
8 In Vain-glory hatcht & nurst
By double Spectres Self Accurst
My Son! my Son! thou treatest me
But as I have instructed thee
9 On the shadows of the Moon
Climbing thro Nights highest noon
10 In Times Ocean falling drownd
In Aged Ignorance profound.
11 Holy & cold I clipd the Wings
Of all Sublunary Things
12 And in depths of my Dungeons
Closed the Father & the Sons
13 But when once I did descry
The Immortal Man that cannot Die
14 Thro evening shades I haste away
To close the Labours of my Day
15 The Door of Death I open found
And the Worm Weaving in the Ground
16 Thou'rt my Mother from the Womb
Wife, Sister, Daughter to the Tomb
Weaving to Dreams the Sexual strife
And weeping over the Web of Life

To The Accuser who is
The God of This World

Truly My Satan thou art but a Dunce
And dost not know the Garment from the Man
Every Harlot was a Virgin once
Nor canst thou ever change Kate into Nan

Tho thou art Worshipd by the Names Divine
Of Jesus & Jehovah: thou art still
The Son of Morn in weary Nights decline
The lost Travellers Dream under the Hill

19.

LETTERS

FROM THE LETTERS OF
WILLIAM BLAKE

LETTER TO WILLIAM HAYLEY
6 May 1800

Dear Sir,

I am very sorry for your immense loss, which is a repetition of what all feel in this valley of misery & happiness mixed. I send the Shadow of the departed Angel: hope the likeness is improved. The lip I have again lessened as you advised & done a good many other softenings to the whole. I know that our deceased friends are more really with us than when they were apparent to our mortal part. Thirteen years ago I lost a brother & with his spirit I converse daily & hourly in the Spirit & See him in my remembrance in the regions of my Imagination. I hear his advice & even now write from his Dictate. Forgive me for Expressing to you my Enthusiasm which I wish all to partake of Since it is to me a Source of Immortal Joy: even in this world by it I am the companion of Angels. May you continue to be so more & more & to be more & more perswaded that every Mortal loss is an Immortal Gain. The Ruins of Time builds Mansions in Eternity.—I have also sent A Proof of Pericles for your Remarks, thanking you for the Kindness with which you Express them & feeling heartily your Grief with a brother's Sympathy.

I remain, Dear Sir, Your humble Servant

William Blake

Lambeth. May 6. 1800

LETTER TO JOHN FLAXMAN
21 September 1800

Dear Sculptor of Eternity,

We are safe arrived at our Cottage, which is more beautiful than I thought it, & more convenient. It is a perfect Model for Cottages &, I think, for Palaces of Magnificence, only Enlarging, not altering its proportions & adding ornaments & not principals. Nothing can be more Grand than its Simplicity & Usefulness. Simple without Intricacy, it seems to be the Spontaneous Effusion of Humanity congenial to the wants of Man. No other formed House can ever please me so well; nor shall I ever be perswaded, I believe, that it can be improved either in Beauty or Use.

Mr Hayley reciev'd us with his usual brotherly affection. I have begun to work. Felpham is a sweet place for Study, because it is more Spiritual than London. Heaven opens here on all sides her Golden Gates; her windows are not obstructed by vapours; voices of Celestial inhabitants are more distinctly heard, & their forms more distinctly seen, & my Cottage is also a Shadow of their houses. My Wife & Sister are both well, courting Neptune for an Embrace.

Our Journey was very pleasant; & tho' we had a great deal of Luggage, No Grumbling, All was Chearfulness & Good Humour on the Road, & yet we could not arrive at our Cottage before half past Eleven at night, owing to the necessary shifting of our Luggage from one Chaise to another; for we had Seven Different Chaises, & as many different drivers. We set out between Six & Seven in the Morning of Thursday, with Sixteen heavy boxes & portfolios full of prints. And Now Begins a New life, because another covering of Earth is shaken off. I am more famed in Heaven for my works than I could well concieve. In my Brain are studies & Chambers fill'd with books & pictures of old, which I wrote & painted in ages of Eternity before my mortal life; & those works are the delight & Study of Archangels. Why, then, should I be anxious about the riches or fame of mortality. The Lord our father will do for us & with us according to his Divine will for our Good.

You, O Dear Flaxman, are a Sublime Archangel, My Friend & Companion from Eternity; in the Divine bosom in our Dwelling place. I look back into the regions of Reminiscence & behold our ancient days before this Earth appear'd in its vegetated mortality to my mortal vegetated Eyes. I see our houses of Eternity, which can never be separated, tho' our Mortal vehicles should stand at the remotest corners of heaven from each other.

Farewell, My Best Friend. Remember Me & My Wife in Love & Friendship to our Dear Mrs Flaxman, whom we ardently desire to Entertain beneath our thatched roof of rusted gold, & believe me for ever to remain

Your Grateful & Affectionate,
William Blake

Felpham
Septr 21, 1800
Sunday Morning

from LETTER TO THOMAS BUTTS
10 January 1802

Felpham Jany 10. 1802

Dear Sir,

. . . The Thing I have most at Heart—more than life, or all that seems to make life comfortable without—Is the Interest of True Religion & Science, & whenever any thing appears to affect that Interest (Especially if I myself omit any duty to my Station as a Soldier of Christ), It gives me the greatest of torments. I am not ashamed, afraid, or averse to tell you what Ought to be Told: That I am under the direction of Messengers from Heaven, Daily & Nightly; but the nature of such things is not, as some suppose, without trouble or care. Temptations are on the right hand & left; behind, the sea of time & space roars & follows swiftly; he who keeps not right onward is lost, & if our footsteps slide in clay, how can we do otherwise than fear & tremble? but I should not have troubled You with this account of my spiritual state, unless it had been necessary in explaining the actual cause of my uneasiness, into which you are so kind as to Enquire; for I never obtrude such things on others unless question'd, & then I never disguise the truth.—But if we fear to do the dictates of our Angels, & tremble at the Tasks set before us; if we refuse to do Spiritual Acts because of Natural Fears or Natural Desires! Who can describe the dismal torments of such a state! —I too well remember the Threats I heard!— If you, who are organized by Divine Providence for Spiritual communion, Refuse, & bury your Talent in the Earth, even tho' you should want Natural Bread, Sorrow & Desperation pursues you thro' life, & after death shame & confusion of face to eternity. Every one in Eternity will leave you, aghast at the Man who was crown'd with glory & honour by his brethren, & betray'd their cause to their enemies. You will be call'd the base Judas who betray'd his Friend!—Such words would make any stout man tremble, & how then could I be at ease? But I am now no longer in That State, & now go on again with my Task, Fearless, and tho' my path is difficult, I have no fear of stumbling while I keep it.

My wife desires her kindest Love to Mrs Butts, & I have permitted her to send it to you also; we often wish that we could unite again in Society, & hope that the time is not distant when we shall do so, being determin'd not to remain another winter here, but to return to London.

I hear a voice you cannot hear, that says I must not stay,
I see a hand you cannot see, that beckons me away.

Naked we came here, naked of Natural things, & naked we shall return; but while cloth'd with the Divine Mercy, we are richly cloth'd in Spiritual & suffer all the rest gladly. Pray give my Love to Mrs Butts & your family.
I am, Yours Sincerely,

William Blake

LETTER TO THOMAS BUTTS
25 April 1803

My Dear Sir,

I write in haste, having reciev'd a pressing Letter from my Brother. I intended to have sent the Picture of the Riposo, which is nearly finish'd much to my satisfaction, but not quite; you shall have it soon. I now send the 4 Numbers for Mr Birch, with best Respects to him. The Reason the Ballads have been suspended is the pressure of other business, but they will go on again soon.

Accept of my thanks for your kind & heartening Letter. You have Faith in the Endeavours of Me, your weak brother & fellow Disciple; how great must be your faith in our Divine Master! You are to me a Lesson of Humility, while you Exalt me by such distinguishing commendations. I know that you see certain merits in me, which, by God's Grace, shall be made fully apparent & perfect in Eternity; in the mean time I must not bury the Talents in the Earth, but do my endeavour to live to the Glory of our Lord & Saviour; & I am also grateful to the kind hand that endeavours to lift me out of despondency, even if it lifts me too high.

And now, My Dear Sir, Congratulate me on my return to London, with the full approbation of Mr Hayley & with Promise—But, Alas!

Now I may say to you, what perhaps I should not dare to say to any one else: That I can alone carry on my visionary studies in London unannoy'd, & that I may converse with my friends in Eternity, See Visions, Dream Dreams & prophecy & speak Parables unobserv'd & at liberty from the Doubts of other Mortals; perhaps Doubts proceeding from Kindness, but Doubts are always pernicious, Especially when we Doubt our Friends. Christ is very decided on this Point: 'He who is Not With Me is Against Me.' There is no Medium or Middle state; & if a Man is the Enemy of my Spiritual Life while he pretends to be the Friend of my Corporeal, he is a Real Enemy—but the Man may be the friend of my Spiritual Life while he seems the Enemy of my Corporeal, but Not Vice Versa.

What is very pleasant, Every one who hears of my going to London again Applauds it as the only course for the interest of all concern'd in My Works, Observing that I ought not to be away from the opportunities London affords of seeing fine Pictures, and the various improvements in Works of Art going on in London.

But none can know the Spiritual Acts of my three years' Slumber on the banks of the Ocean, unless he has seen them in the Spirit, or unless he should read My long Poem descriptive of those Acts; for I have in these three years composed an immense number of verses on One Grand Theme, Similar to Homer's Iliad or Milton's Paradise Lost, the Persons & Machinery intirely new to the Inhabitants of Earth (some of the Persons Excepted). I have written this Poem from immediate Dictation, twelve or sometimes twenty or thirty lines at a time, without Premeditation & even against my Will; the Time it has taken in writing was thus render'd Non Existent, & an immense Poem Exists which seems to be the Labour of a long Life, all produc'd without Labour or Study. I mention this to shew you what I think the Grand Reason of my being brought down here.

I have a thousand & ten thousand things to say to you. My heart is full of futurity. I percieve that the sore travel which has been given me these three years leads to Glory & Honour. I rejoice & I tremble: 'I am fearfully & wonderfully made.' I had been reading the cxxxix Psalm a little before your Letter arrived. I take your advice. I see the face of my Heavenly Father; he lays his Hand upon my Head & gives a blessing to all my works; why should I be troubled? why should my heart & flesh cry out? I will go on in the Strength of the Lord; through Hell will I sing forth his Praises, that the Dragons of the Deep may praise him, & that those who dwell in darkness & in the Sea coasts may be gather'd into his Kingdom. Excuse my, perhaps, too great Enthusiasm. Please to accept of & give our Loves to Mrs Butts & your amiable Family, & believe me to be,

Ever Yours Affectionately,

Will Blake

Felpham
April 25. 1803

LETTER TO WILLIAM HAYLEY
7 October 1803

London, October 7, 1803.

Dear Sir,

Your generous & tender solicitude about your devoted rebel makes it absolutely necessary that he should trouble you with an account of his safe arrival, which will excuse his begging the favor of a few lines to inform him how you escaped the contagion of the Court of Justice—I fear that you have & must suffer more on my account than I shall ever be worth—Arrived safe in London, my wife in very poor health, still I resolve not to lose hope of seeing better days.

Art in London flourishes. Engravers in particular are wanted. Every Engraver turns away work that he cannot execute from his superabundant Employment. Yet no one brings work to me. I am content that it shall be so as long as God pleases. I know that many works of a lucrative nature are in want of hands; other Engravers are courted. I suppose that I must go a Courting, which I shall do awkwardly; in the mean time I lose no moment to complete Romney to satisfaction.

How is it possible that a Man almost 50 Years of Age, who has not lost any of his life since he was five years old without incessant labour & study, how is it possible that such a one with ordinary common sense can be inferior to a boy of twenty, who scarcely has taken or deigns to take a pencil in hand, but who rides about the Parks or Saunters about the Playhouses, who Eats & drinks for business not for need, how is it possible that such a fop can be superior to the studious lover of Art can scarcely be imagin'd. Yet such is somewhat like my fate & such it is likely to remain. Yet I laugh & sing, for if on Earth neglected I am in heaven a Prince among Princes, & even on Earth beloved by the Good as a Good Man; this I should be perfectly contented with, but at certain periods a blaze of reputation arises round me in which I am consider'd as one distinguish'd by some mental perfection, but the flame soon dies again & I am left stupified and astonish'd. O that I could live as others do in a regular succession of Employment, this wish I fear is not to be accomplish'd to me—Forgive this Dirge-like lamentation over a dead horse, & now I have lamented over the dead horse let me laugh & be merry with my friends till Christmas, for as Man liveth not by bread alone, I shall live altho' I should want bread—nothing is necessary to me but to do my Duty & to rejoice in the exceeding joy that is always poured out on my Spirit, to pray that my friends & you above the rest may be made partakers of the joy that the world cannot concieve, that you may still be replenish'd with the same & be as you always have been, a glorious & triumphant Dweller in immortality. Please to pay for me my best thanks to Miss Poole: tell her that I wish her a continued Excess of Happiness—some say that Happiness is not Good for Mortals, & they ought to be answer'd that Sorrow is not fit for Immortals & is utterly useless to any one; a blight never does good to a tree, & if a blight kill not a tree but it still bear fruit, let none say that the fruit was in consequence of the blight. When this Soldier-like danger is over I will do double the work I do now, for it will hang heavy on my Devil who terribly resents it; but I soothe him to peace, & indeed he is a good natur'd Devil after all & certainly does not lead me into scrapes—he is not in the least to be blamed for the present scrape, as he was out of the way all the time on other employment seeking amusement in making Verses, to which he constantly leads me very much to my hurt & sometimes to the annoyance of my friends; as I percieve he is now doing the same work by my letter, I will finish it, wishing you health & joy in God our Saviour.

To Eternity yours,
Willm Blake

LETTER TO JOHN LINNELL
February 1827

February, 1827.

Dear Sir,

I thank you for the Five Pounds recieved to day: am getting better every Morning, but slowly, as I am still feeble & tottering, tho' all the Symptoms of my complaint seem almost gone as the fine weather is very beneficial & comfortable to me. I go on, as I think, improving my Engravings of Dante more & more, & shall soon get Proofs of these Four which I have, & beg the favour of you to send me the two Plates of Dante which you have, that I may finish them sufficiently to make some shew of Colour & Strength.

I have thought & thought of the Removal & cannot get my Mind out of a state of terrible fear at such a step; the more I think, the more I feel terror at what I wish'd at first & thought it a thing of benefit & Good hope; you will attribute it to its right Cause—Intellectual Peculiarity, that must be Myself alone shut up in Myself, or Reduced to Nothing. I could tell you of Visions & dreams upon the Subject: I have asked & intreated Divine help, but fear continues upon me, & I must relinquish the step that I had wish'd to take, & still wish, but in vain.

Your Success in your Profession is above all things to me most gratifying; may it go on to the Perfection you wish & more. So wishes also

Yours Sincerely,
William Blake

LETTER TO JOHN LINNELL
25 April 1827

Dear Sir,

I am going on better Every day, as I think, both in health & in work. I thank you for The Ten Pounds which I recieved from you this day, which shall be put to the best use; as also for the prospect of Mr Ottley's advantageous acquaintance. I go on without daring to count on Futurity, which I cannot do without doubt & Fear that ruins Activity, & are the greatest hurt to an Artist such as I am. As to Ugolino, &c, I never supposed that I should sell them; my Wife alone is answerable for their having Existed in any finish'd State. I am too much attach'd to Dante to think much of anything else. I have Proved the Six Plates, & reduced the Fighting devils ready for the Copper. I count myself sufficiently Paid If I live as I now do, & only fear that I may be Unlucky to my friends, & especially that I may not be so to you.

I am, sincerely yours,

William Blake

25 April 1827

Index of Titles

INDEX OF TITLES